Embellishea Fashions

Embellished Fashions

Mickey Baskett

STERLING

New York / London
www.sterlingpublishing.com

Prolific Impressions Production Staff:
Editor in Chief: Mickey Baskett
Copy Editor: Phyllis Mueller
Graphics: Dianne Miller, Karen Turpin
Styling: Lenos Key
Photography: Jerry Mucklow, Joel Tressler
Administration: Jim Baskett

Every effort has been made to insure that the information presented is accurate. Since we have no control over physical conditions, individual skills, or chosen tools and products, the publisher disclaims any liability for injuries, losses, untoward results, or any other damages which may result from the use of the information in this book. Thoroughly read the instructions for all products used to complete the projects in this book, paying particular attention to all cautions and warnings shown for that product to ensure their proper and safe use.

Library of Congress Cataloging-in-Publication Data

Baskett, Mickey.
 Embellished fashions / Mickey Baskett.
    p. cm.
 Includes index.
 ISBN-13: 978-1-4027-4433-4
 ISBN-10: 1-4027-4433-1
 1. Fancy work. 2. Textile crafts. 3. Clothing and dress. I. Title.

TT751.B227 2007
746.4--dc22

2007018139

2 4 6 8 10 9 7 5 3 1

Published by Sterling Publishing Co., Inc.
387 Park Avenue South, New York, NY 10016
©2008 by Prolific Impressions, Inc.
Distributed in Canada by Sterling Publishing
c/o Canadian Manda Group, 165 Dufferin Street,
Toronto, Ontario, Canada M6K 3H6
Distributed in the United Kingdom by GMC Distribution Services,
Castle Place, 166 High Street, Lewes, East Sussex, England BN7 1XU
Distributed in Australia by Capricorn Link (Australia) Pty. Ltd.
P.O. Box 704, Windsor, NSW 2756, Australia

Printed in China
All rights reserved

ISBN-13: 978-1-4027-4433-4
ISBN-10: 1-4027-4433-1

For information about custom editions, special sales, premium and corporate purchases, please contact Sterling Special Sales Department at 800-805-5489 or specialsales@sterlingpub.com.

Acknowledgements

Thank you to the following manufacturers for supplying product to use in the making of these garments:

Beacon Chemical Company, Inc., 125 MacQuesten Parkway South, Mount Vernon, NY 10550, for Gem-Tac glue

Creative Crystal Company, (*www.creative-crystal.com*) for the BeJeweler™ Tool and Swarovski® crystals.

The DMC Corporation, 77 South Hackensack Av, Bldg 10F, South Kearny, NJ 07032 for embroidery floss

Jill MacKay, *www.JillMacKay.com* for sterling silver Beadable Embellishments.

Plaid Enterprises, Inc., *www.plaidonline.com* for FolkArt® Fabric Paint & Jean-e-ology™ Iron-on Trims.

Provo Crafts, *www.provocraft.com* for PattieWack Pompom Templates.

This book is dedicated to all the designers who have ever stayed up all night restyling your clothes or sewing sequins on a blouse because you couldn't purchase the exact look you needed for the big occasion the next day.

A special thanks to the following designers who are so beautifully gifted in working with their hands:
- *Patty Cox*
- *Miche Baskett*
- *Phyllis Dobbs*
- *Pattie Donham*
- *Cindy Gorder*
- *Sue Penrod*

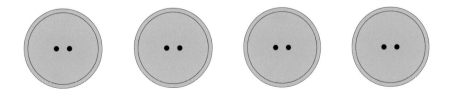

CONTENTS

Introduction

It seems that humans have *always* had a desire to "guild the lily," adorn themselves, embellish the plain. Even Eve couldn't leave well enough alone – she just had to find a fig leaf to wear. From the indigenous peoples, to the Romans, Egyptians, Greeks – and all the way to modern man – beads, colorful threads, paint, and more are used to create beautiful designs on our clothing as well as our bodies. History shows us that native peoples from all continents used dyes or paint, beads, bone, feathers, shells, or other items that were of beauty to them to decorate themselves for war, marriage, and other auspicious times. As early as 30BC Romans used glass rings and beads to embellish their clothing. Egyptians seemed to take the art of embellishment to its height. Findings in some of the Egyptian burial sits include personal adornments such as ebony, gemstones, and metal jewelry; Kohl tubes that were used to decorate the eyes; and burial shrouds decorated with amulets of precious stone and gold beads. So I guess you could say "it comes by us naturally" – our long history of desiring to beautify ourselves and our clothing.

There are so many different techniques available to us for embellishing our clothing – embroidery, appliqué, paint, beading, cutwork, adding ribbons and trims, crochet. And the products from which we can choose are astounding. "So many choices, so little time" is an expression that rings true when it comes to ways to decorate our wearables. In this book, I have tried to touch upon some quick and easy ways you can inexpensively restyle garments from plain to beautiful – without having to be an expert at any one technique. The products offered today had a big influence in my decisions of what techniques to include in this book. I wanted to make sure you could find the same type of products to use to recreate garments similar to the ones you see in the following pages.

Look at any fashion magazine, clothing catalog, or clothing store and you will notice t-shirts with beaded necklines, jeans and jackets encrusted with sequins and jewels, embroidered dresses – tassels, fringe, studs, ribbons, braid. But the price tags for these gorgeous garments may not be user friendly. However, with the instructions in this book you can recreate some of these same looks for a fraction of the cost. So scour your closets, or visit a favorite consignment, thrift shop, or a nearby discount store for generic wearables that can be a blank canvas for embellishment. There is nothing as gratifying as restyling a $5.00 jacket into a chic *haute couture* look-alike that would cost several hundred dollars. There's a plain t-shirt out there just waiting for you to make it pretty. ○

Chapter 1

Embellishing with Beads & Jewels

Beads and jewels add three-dimensional texture, metallic shine, and sparkle. The techniques for applying them vary according to the type of embellishment you choose. Beads and jewels can be glued in place with jewel glue or fabric paint; beads can be sewn with beading thread. There are iron-on rhinestones and studs, jewels and studs that require a mechanical setting tool, and hot-fix adhesive-backed jewels that are attached with a hot-fix applicator. This chapter will introduce you to many of the types of gems that are available and how to use them.

General Supplies & Instructions

Jewels & Rhinestones

Jewels and rhinestones (together referred to as "gems") have faceted or domed faces and flat backs, which makes them ideal for embellishing flat surfaces. They may be made of glass or acrylic. Gems typically don't have holes for beading or sewing and are secured in place with glue or dimensional fabric paint.

Sequins

Sequins, loose, come in packages or strung on thread. They are more secure and look best if they are stitched in place; but they can be glued as well.

Tweezers

Use tweezers to precisely place rhinestones, nail heads, or studs.

Attaching Gems with Jewel Glue

Use jewel glue for attaching rhinestones, gems, mirrors, pearls, and other embellishments. Also called embellishment glue or jewel adhesive, it is permanent, water-based, non-toxic, washable, and clear-drying. There are two methods for attaching the gems. One way is to simply hold the embellishment with a pair of tweezers, place a dot of glue on the back, and put in place. Another way is to put the glue on the fabric.

1. Squeeze a dot of glue on the fabric where you want to place the stone or stud.

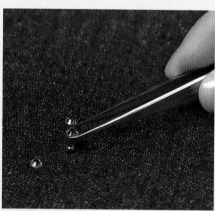

2. Pick up the embellishment with tweezers and place it over the glue. Don't move the fabric until the glue dries.

Attaching Gems with Fabric Paint

Dimensional fabric paint, which comes in squeeze bottles in an array of colors including metallics and glitters, is an easy, very durable attachment for all kinds of flat-backed pearls, studs, and jewels. You simply apply paint to the back of the gem and position the gem on the garment.

There are two methods for attaching gems with dimensional fabric paint. With one method, no paint shows; with the other, you use more paint so that when the gem is positioned and pressed into place, some paint oozes out around the sides of the gem and creates a bezel around it. (This technique works best on round gems.) *TIP: It's a good idea to practice on a scrap piece of fabric to get a feel for the amount of paint to use.*

Photo 1 – Squeezing a dot of paint on the back.

Photo 2 – Pressing the gem into place.

Photo 3 – Making an evenly spaced row of gems.

Photo 4 – Using tweezers to place a small gem.

To attach gems with no paint showing:

1. Squeeze paint on center of the back of the gem. Don't cover the entire back of the gem; instead, squeeze paint in the center of the gem, allowing a margin around the dot of paint. (Photo 1)
2. Position the gem and push down slightly to secure it in place. (Photo 2)
3. To make a row of gems with the same amount of space between each one, cut a piece of card stock as wide as the space you want between the gems. After placing the first gem, place the spacer beside it, then place the second gem. (Photo 3)
4. If gems are too small to hold, use tweezers to place the gems. (Photo 4)

To make a bezel around a gem:

1. Squeeze paint on the back of the gem, applying it around the perimeter and up to the edge. (Photo 5)
2. Place the gem and press down evenly so that paint oozes out from under the gem and creates a rim around the gem similar to a bezel in fine jewelry. (Photo 6)
3. If the paint does not ooze out evenly or if there's not enough paint to ooze out, use the writer tip to make a line of paint around the gem. (Photo 7)

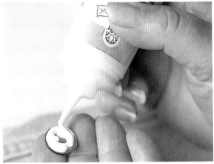

Photo 5 – Covering the back of the gem with paint.

Photo 6 – Pressing the gem into place and creating the paint bezel.

Photo 7 – Using the tip to outline the gem with paint.

Attaching Hot Fix Jewels

Hot Fix Applicator Tool

There are several models available that are used to heat and melt the adhesive on the back of hot-fix gems. This means that the gems have adhesive on the back of them that is melted with the tool. Most applicators come with a variety of tips to accommodate the various sizes of stones so that the stone can be picked up and placed with this tip. If you don't have a tip to fit a stone you are using, you can place the stone with tweezers. When the stones are in place, the tool is pressed onto the face of the stone until the adhesive has melted. You can also use the applicator to attach self-adhesive nail heads and studs – place them with tweezers, then heat them with the tool. Follow manufacturer's recommendations for the amount of time to press the tip onto the stone.

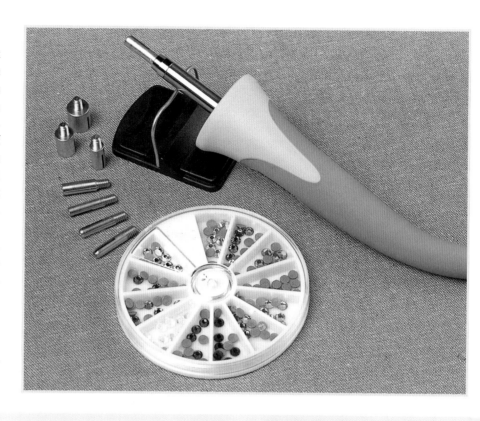

1. *Place the appropriate-size tip on the applicator tool. Plug in the tool. Place the garment on a firm, flat surface. Place the rhinestones, face up, on a hard, flat surface. Pick up a stone with the applicator tool.*

2. *Wait a few seconds. The heat-sensitive glue on the bottom of the stone will begin to melt and shine. (The glue on smaller stones takes less time to melt.)*

3. *As soon as the glue looks shiny, place the loaded applicator straight down on the fabric. Allow the stone – but not the applicator tip – to touch the fabric. The stone will release from the applicator and attach to the fabric. Lift the tool immediately.*

Beads & Pearls

Beads are made all over the world and can be found at crafts stores and the notions departments of variety and department stores. There are literally hundred of styles and shapes from which to choose. Beads are made in a variety of materials, including glass, wood, ceramic, metal, acrylic, semi-precious stones, clay, and natural minerals. They are classified according to material, shape, and size. Most beads have holes for stringing and can be sewn in place. Their sizes are generally measured in millimeters (mm).

Most **pearls** are round beads with an iridescent coating. **Seed beads** are small, rounded glass beads that are oblate in shape (fatter in diameter than they are long). They are also called **E beads** or **rocaille beads**. E beads are usually larger seed beads. Bugle beads are tubular-shaped glass beads. **Faceted beads** are made of molded glass or plastic. They have flattened, ground, cut, or polished reflective surfaces called facets. They are usually transparent.

Beading Needles & Thread

Beading needles come in a range of sizes – the higher size numbers denote smaller needles. Size 12 needles will work for most size 11 (the most common size) or larger seed beads. Size 15 seed beads require size 15 needles. Having an assortment of lengths will come in handy – often a short needle is easier to control in a tight or curved space. Long needles are great for making tassels. And medium needles are pretty universal in their utility. TIP: Take the time to test a few beads before anchoring thread to fabric to be sure you're using a needle that's small enough for the beads you've chosen.

Beading threads are sold in several sizes and colors. You need only two colors – black and white – for just about any bead-on-fabric situation. Some threads come already waxed; others should be waxed with beeswax or **thread wax** to keep it from tangling as you work.

Beading thread, needles, and thread wax

Beads & Jewels

Micro Beads

Tiny round **glass** beads with no holes can add beautiful glitter to your fashion accessories. They come in vials or packages and are adhered to surfaces with glue, fabric dimensional paint, or an extra-sticky double-sided tape made especially for that purpose. Micro beads are recommended for use only on items that do not require laundering such as purses, jewelry, or shoes.

Using the tape:

1. Pour the micro beads into a bowl or container that will hold the beads and keep them from spilling. Apply the sticky tape to the item where you want the beads to be. (Photo 1)
2. Pull off the backing from the tape. (Photo 2)
3. Press the taped area into the container of beads. (Photo 3) The beads will nicely cover the tape to create glitter and shine. (Photo 4)

Using dimensional fabric paint:

Beads can also be sprinkled on wet dimensional paint. (Photo 5)

Photo 1 – Applying the tape.

Photo 2 – Pulling off the backing paper.

Photo 3 – Pressing the taped area into the container of beads.

Photo 4 – The area is covered with beads.

Photo 5 – Sprinkling beads over wet dimensional paint.

Pearl Power Blouse

Though the pearls may look randomly placed, they actually have an exact, measured placement – 1" apart, when possible. Sometimes the measurement had to be varied; for example, as the collar narrows, the rows are a little closer together, but the spacing of the pearls along the row is still 1" apart.

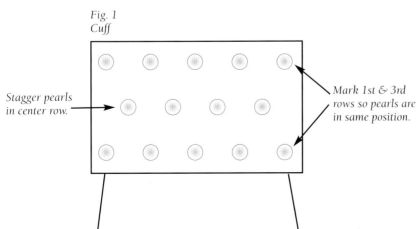

Fig. 1
Cuff

Stagger pearls in center row.

Mark 1st & 3rd rows so pearls are in same position.

SUPPLIES

Base:

White blouse with collar and long cuffed sleeves

Embellishments:

125 (approx.) white pearls, 8mm

Tools & Other Supplies:

Sewing needle

White thread

Ruler

Fabric marker, disappearing or washable

Scissors

INSTRUCTIONS

1. Remove the buttons from the button placket. (They will be replaced with pearls.)
2. With a fabric marker, make dots on the bottom edge of the collar 1" apart. Make dots along the top edge of the collar 1" apart in the same positions as the dots along the bottom. Measure the distance between these two rows and make a center row of dots between them, placing these dots 1" apart at an equal distance between the two rows and staggered between the dots on the first and third rows.
3. Mark the cuffs the same way. If your cuffs aren't big enough for three rows 1" apart, adjust the measurements, but don't place the rows closer than 1" apart.
4. Mark the button placket and the top edge of the pocket, using the same 1" spacing.
5. Securely sew a pearl to the blouse at each dot. ○

Jeweled Moccasins

You can use this idea to add sparkling embellishments to moccasins, deck shoes, or any plain-toe shoes.

by Patty Cox

Fig. 1 –
Placement diagram

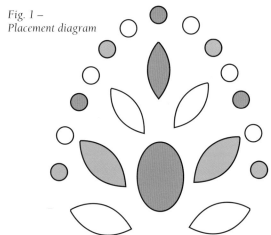

SUPPLIES

Base:
Moccasins, deck shoes, or plain-toe shoes

Embellishments:
4 clear navette* faceted jewels,
  18mm x 8mm
4 turquoise navette faceted jewels,
  18mm x 8mm
4 clear navette faceted jewels,
  7mm x 16mm
2 blue navette faceted jewels,
  7mm x 16mm
2 blue oval cabochons, 14mm x 18mm
Rhinestones, 5mm – 12 clear, 8 light
  blue, 6 dark blue
1-2/3 yds. turquoise organza ribbon,
  3/8" wide
3/4 yd. blue organza ribbon, 3/4" wide

*navette-shaped gems are marquise or
football-shaped gems.*

Tools & Other Supplies:
Needle with long, large eye
Jewel glue
Fray preventive (sold in sewing
  departments)

INSTRUCTIONS

1. Arrange and glue the stones in position on the toe areas of the shoes, using permanent jewel adhesive. See Fig. 1.
2. Cut two 30" pieces of 3/8" turquoise organza ribbon. Thread one piece through the large eye needle. Starting at shoe front, thread ribbon through the eyelets of the shoe. Bring the ribbon ends to the front of the shoe. Knot the ribbon. Repeat on the other shoe.
3. Cut two 13¹/₂" pieces of 3/4" blue organza ribbon. Tie each piece of ribbon in a bow. Apply fray preventive liquid to the cut ends.
4. Glue or tie bows on shoes at center front. ○

Moccasins with Shells & Beads

The shell and bead designs on these moccasins give the shoes a natural, Native American style.

by Patty Cox

Fig. 1 –
Placement diagram

SUPPLIES

Base:
Moccasins, deck shoes, or plain-toe shoes

Embellishments:
10 cowrie shells
12 turquoise e beads
1-2/3 yd. ecru organza ribbon, 1/4" wide
3/4" yd. ecru organza ribbon, 3/4" wide

Tools & Other Supplies:
Jewel glue
Sharp needle
Beading thread
Fray preventive

1. Arrange and glue shells and beads in position on the toe areas of the shoes, using permanent jewel adhesive.
2. Thread needle with beading thread. Knot end. Secure beads and shells with beading thread. On the cowrie shells, stitch over the center opening. Knot the thread inside the shoes.
3. Cut two 30" pieces of 1/4" organza ribbon. Thread one 30" piece through the large eye needle. Starting at the shoe front, thread ribbon through the eyelets of the shoe. Bring the ribbon end to the front of the shoe. Knot the ribbon. Repeat on the other shoe.
4. Cut two 13¹/₂" pieces of 3/4" organza ribbon. Tie each piece of ribbon in a bow. Apply fray preventive liquid to the cut ends.
5. Glue or tie bow on shoes at center front. ○

Snowflake Jeans

SUPPLIES

Base:

Denim jeans

Embellishments:

Navette* crystal rhinestones,
   18mm x 8mm

Navette crystal rhinestones,
   15mm x 7mm

Round crystal rhinestones, 5mm

Round crystal rhinestones, 7mm

Round crystal rhinestones, 9mm

Silver-lined bugle beads, size 5

Twisted silver-lined bugle beads, size 3

Silver-lined seed beads, 11/0

Tools & Other Supplies:

Beading thread

Beading needle

Jewel glue

Chalk

navette-shaped gems are marquise or football-shaped gems.

Rhinestones, applied in snowflake motifs, add the sparkle of a winter wonderland to jeans.
Snowflake patterns appear on page 20.

by Patty Cox

INSTRUCTIONS

1. Decide where you'd like to place the snowflakes. (Ours are around the front pockets and on the bottom of one leg.
2. With chalk, mark the placement of the snowflakes, using the Six Point pattern.
3. Using the snowflake patterns as guides, glue rhinestones and beads on the chalk lines, using permanent jewel adhesive. Allow glue to dry.
4. Using a beading needle and thread, secure the bugle beads and seed beads to the jeans. ❍

Transferring Patterns

Here's an easy method for transferring patterns to denim. You'll need tracing paper, a pencil, bridal tulle fabric, a fine tip permanent marker, and light-colored chalk.

Trace the pattern: Trace the pattern from the book, using tracing paper and a pencil. Enlarge on a photocopier to desired size. Place a piece of bridal tulle over the pattern.

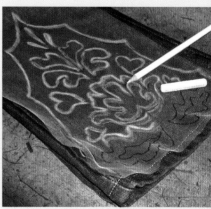

Transfer the design: Position the tulle pattern over the denim. Go over the pattern lines with white chalk (for temporary lines) or a fine-tip permanent marker (for permanent lines).

Snowflake Jeans

Patterns

See page 18 for instructions.

Six Point Pattern

Gem Monogram Bag

Patterns

See page 22 for instructions.

Enlarge to size to fit purse.

ABCDE
FGHIJK
LMNOP
QRSTU
VWXYZ

Gem Monogram Bag

Any plain bag can be personalized by gluing on jewels. Create a handbag that is a designer made one-of-a-kind.

by Patty Cox

SUPPLIES

Base:
Small black bag

Embellishments:
Multi-colored round rhinestones, 5mm
Multi-colored round cabochons, 5mm
Multi-colored round rhinestones, 7mm

Tools & Other Supplies:
Jewel glue
Transfer paper and stylus
Tweezers

INSTRUCTIONS

1. Choose a letter and, using the patterns provided, enlarge the letter to fit your bag (See page 21).
2. Transfer the pattern to the bag using transfer paper.
3. Squeeze a small puddle of glue on a piece of scrap paper. Pick up a stone with tweezers and dip the flat bottom in glue. Position stone on bag. Arrange and glue all stones to fit in the pattern area. ○

Natural Bead Tee

Wooden beads are sewn around the neckline of a simple t-shirt, giving the look of a necklace. Use pairs of beads for a symmetrical (mirror image) arrangement as we did, or place assorted beads randomly.

by Miche Baskett

SUPPLIES

Base:

V-neck t-shirt *or* lightweight sweater

Embellishments:

50 (approx.) wooden beads, 1/4" to 1/2" – Various shades

Tools & Other Supplies:

Embroidery floss to match shirt

Beading needle

Scissors

INSTRUCTIONS

1. Arrange half the beads in a pleasing pattern, using the photo as a guide.
2. Starting with the center bead at the point of the V-neck, begin sewing beads on the shirt with the matching embroidery floss. Use a back stitch, working along the neckline, adding one bead at a time until you reach the shoulder seam. Tie off the thread inside the shirt.
3. Sew beads to the other side of the neckline, matching the sequence on the first side. ○

Dressed Up Denim Jacket

SUPPLIES

Base:

Denim jacket

Embellishments:

36 (approx.) flat-backed jewels,
    25mm to 8mm

4 yds. strung red sequins (or enough
    to trim your jacket edges)

Tools & Other Supplies:

Dimensional fabric paints – Gold
    glitter, red glitter, blue glitter

Jewel glue

A fitted denim jacket with a rounded peplum is jeweled up with flat-backed gems, dimensional fabric paint, and sequins. We used flat-backed jewels in a variety of colors and attached and outlined them with gold glitter dimensional paint.

INSTRUCTIONS

1. Plan the spacing and positioning of the jewels on the jacket.
2. Attach all the jewels to jacket using gold glitter dimensional paint. Use the photo as a guide for placement. Don't put a lot of paint on the back of the jewel – you don't want the paint to ooze out from underneath the jewel when it is placed.
3. After placing each jewel on jacket, outline it with gold glitter dimensional paint, using the applicator tip of the paint bottle.
4. Randomly place dots or dashes of red glitter paint and blue glitter paint around the jewels. Allow to dry undisturbed overnight.
5. Cut pieces of sequin rope to go along the edge of the peplum and around each cuff. Glue in place with fabric glue. Let dry. ◯

Gluing on Gems

The bezels around the gems were added after the gems were glued in place. Because the gems were a variety of shapes, the technique of adding enough paint to ooze out around them when pushed down does not work. That technique is best on round gems. Here we added just a dot of glue on the back of the gem and placed it. The writer tip was used to outline each gem.

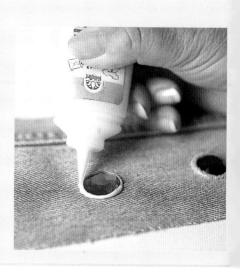

Bejeweled Belts

Embellished belts make elegant accessories. By changing the belt on a garment you vary the look. The studs, pearls, and gems on these belts were attached with dimensional fabric paint, which creates a durable, permanent bond. The amounts of embellishments listed are for a medium size belt – you may need more or fewer jewels or studs. For best results, practice these gluing techniques on a piece of paper. That way, you'll get a feel for the amount of paint you need to apply to the backs of the gems and studs for best results.

Jeweled Belt
SUPPLIES

Base:
Leather belt, at least 1¼" wide

Embellishments:
30 (approx.) flat-backed jewels, 20mm round and 12mm square, colors of your choice
Dimensional fabric paint – Silver metallic

Tools & Other Supplies:
Scissors
Scrap of paper *or* cardboard

INSTRUCTIONS

1. Determine how you wish to space the gems on your belt, adjusting the amount of space between them until the result pleases you. The gems on our belt are placed in a pattern of alternating squares and rounds with 3/16" of space between each gem. *TIP:* Cut a piece of paper or cardboard to use as a spacer tool.
2. Attach all the gems to the belt with dimensional fabric paint. Squeeze enough paint onto the back of the gems so that when they are placed and pushed down slightly, a margin of paint oozes out from under the gems and creates a rim around the gem. *TIP:* If enough paint does not ooze out from under the gem to create a rim, you can make a bead of paint around the gem after it is attached.
3. Add dots of silver paint to the loop.
4. Let dry overnight. ○

Pearl & Stud Belt
SUPPLIES

Base:
Leather belt, at least 1¼" wide

Embellishments:
Choose glue-on type studs without prongs.
6 marquise-shaped gold metal studs, 10mm long
5 (approx.) oval gold metal studs, 15mm long
12 (approx.) oval gold metal studs, 10mm long
10 (approx.) flat-backed round pearl jewels, 15mm
Dimensional fabric paint – Gold metallic
1 vial gold micro beads (the tiny ones with no holes)

Tools & Other Supplies:
Double-sided very sticky tape
Scissors
Paper *or* cardboard
Container, such as a small box

INSTRUCTIONS
Create the Pattern:
1. Determine how you wish to space the pearls and studs. Begin with three marquise studs at the buckle end. Move toward the tongue end, creating a pattern with one pearl, one 15mm metal oval stud, one pearl, and three 10mm metal oval studs. Repeat the pattern until you are near the holes at the tongue. Finish with three marquise studs. *TIP:* When spacing the pearls, allow a little extra room to accommodate the paint rim.
2. On this belt, there is 3/16" of space between each gem and stud. Once you determine the correct spacing for the gems on your felt, cut a piece of paper or cardboard the width of the space between the gems to use as a spacer while gluing the gems in place.

Attach the Embellishments:
1. Attach the metal studs and the flat-backed pearls to the belt with dimensional fabric paint in sequence, starting at the buckle end.
   For studs, squeeze a small amount of paint on the back of the stud – you don't want the paint to ooze out from under the stud when it is secured to the belt.
   For pearls, put enough paint on the backs of the pearls so that when they are placed and pushed down slightly, a margin of

paint will ooze out from under the pearl and create a bezel or rim. Immediately sprinkle gold micro beads on the paint rim while wet. Do this as soon as you attach each pearl to assure good adhesion.

2. Allow paint to dry six hours or overnight.

Decorate the Buckle:

1. Pour micro beads into a box or bowl.

2. Apply strips of double-sided sticky tape to the buckle. Remove the liner from the tape.

3. Dip the tape into the beads to cover the tape. ◯

Fiesta Wear

SUPPLIES

Base:

Black t-shirt

Embellishments:

1/2 yd. sheer black fabric

Multi-strand necklace with orange, yellow, and red beads

Flower-shaped earrings to match necklace

Tools & Other Supplies:

Black thread

Chalk pencil

Ruler

Sewing needle

Scissors

Straight pins

Sewing machine

Iron

This richly beaded top started as a plain black t-shirt. The neckline was altered to accommodate a sheer fabric insert. We also altered the sleeves of the shirt for a more fashionable look. The beads that are sewn onto the top are from a necklace and matching earrings set. Because the beads were already strung as a necklace, we simply stitched the strands in place on the garment.

By Miche Baskett

INSTRUCTIONS

Alter the Shirt:

1. To change the sleeves from straight sleeves to capped ones, cut off the bottom hem of each sleeve. Find the center front of each sleeve. From this point, cut the sleeve at an angle, cutting toward the inside seam. Turn under the cut edge, press. Turn under again. Press. Hem.

2. Use the ruler and chalk pencil to mark the area around the neckline that you wish to replace with sheer fabric. Use the photo as a guide. *TIP:* Since straight lines are easier to cut and sew, consider a V-shaped neckline.

3. Cut off the ribbing around the top of the t-shirt. Cut the shirt along the marked lines. Carefully – so you don't stretch the shirt out of shape – turn the shirt inside out.

4. Turn under the cut edge 1/4". Press. Turn under again. Press.

5. Place the sheer fabric over the shirt. Mark an area large enough to cover the cutout area plus 1" extra on all sides to make the insert.

6. Cut out the insert.

7. Place fabric right side down. Turn under all the cut edges and the top 1/4". Turn under again. Press. Hem side edges and top.

8. Turn shirt right side out. Place the sheer fabric insert under the cutout area on the shirt. Pin in place.

9. Machine sew the insert to the shirt.

Embellish:

1. Remove the backs from the earrings. (These were glued and popped off easily.)

2. Cut off the clasp and other findings from the necklace strands. If necessary, tie the ends of the strands so that the beads will stay on the string.

3. Arrange the strands of beads and the earrings on the shirt, using the photo as a guide. Mark the placement for the earrings.

4. Sew the earrings to the shirt.

5. Whipstitch the beaded strands to the shirt. TIP: This works well on the t-shirt fabric; on the sheer fabric, the stitches might be too visible. If this is the case, backstitch the beads, a few at a time, to the sheer fabric. ○

Beaded Diamonds

SUPPLIES

Base:

Top with lace-trimmed *or* plain neck-line

Embellishments:

Shiny metallic seed beads – Blue, silver, orange

Tools & Other Supplies:

Thread to match top

Sewing needle

Optional: Chalk pencil, ruler

INSTRUCTIONS

1. If the neckline of your top has lace trim, determine which part of the lace pattern you want to accent with beads. If the neckline of your top doesn't have lace trim, draw diamond-shaped guidelines with a chalk pencil. See the photo for placement.
2. Thread a needle and knot the end of the thread. Push up the needle from the back at the point you want to begin. Load 10 to 12 seed beads on the thread, then push needle back through from front to back.
3. Make a small stitch, coming up from back to front. Reload needle with beads and push needle back through. Repeat to continue sewing the beads until the design is complete. When finished, knot the thread on the back side. ○

We used a V-neck top with lace trim at the neckline and took design cues from the pattern of the lace, but you could use this embellishing idea to enhance the neckline of any garment, lace-trimmed or not.

by Miche Baskett

Bead Crusted Flip-flops

Inexpensive flip-flops can be made glamorous in no time at all. Very sticky tape and micro beads can instantly turn plastic into glitz.

Micro Beads

SUPPLIES

Base:

Flip-flops with 1/2" wide straps

Embellishments:

Micro glass beads, gold

Glass seed bead and tube bead mixture, gold/bronze

Other Supplies:

1/4" wide very sticky double-sided tape

Container that is flat and large enough to accommodate flip flop straps (such as a shoe box lid)

INSTRUCTIONS

1. Pour the gold micro beads into the container.
2. Apply a strip of double sided tape to one edge of each of the flip flops. Apply another strip of tape right next to the first strip. This covered our straps. Apply another strip of tape if the straps on your flip flops are not covered.
3. Remove the backing from the tape strip.
4. Dip the straps into the beads to cover the sticky tape.
5. Return the gold beads left in the container to the original package. Empty the seed bead/tube bead mixture into the container.
6. Remove the backing from the second tape strip. Dip the straps into the bead mixture until covered. Return the bead mixture to the original package. ○

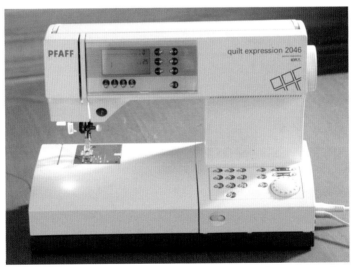

Chapter 2

Embellishing with Fabric Appliqués

Fabric appliqués are shapes cut from fabric and applied by sewing, fusing, or gluing. They can be used as accents or borders or to decorate large areas of a garment or surface.

A sewing machine that makes a smooth, close satin stitch is necessary for making sewn fabric appliqués.

General Information

Attaching Appliqués with Fusible Web

Fusible web is an iron-on adhesive for fabric that you can buy at fabrics stores in packages or by the yard. It has one paper side and one pebbly side. Follow the fusible web manufacturer's instructions for iron temperature and required ironing time.

To make an iron-on applique:

1. Draw or trace the applique design onto the paper side of the fusible web. (Photo 1)
2. Cut out the design from the fusible web with scissors. (Photo 2)

3. Place this paper design, pebbly side down, on the back side of the fabric. Use an iron to fuse the web to the fabric. (Photo 3)
4. Cut out the fabric applique, allowing a slight margin around paper design. (Photo 4)
5. Pull off the paper from the cutout applique. (Photo 5)
6. Place the applique, glue side down, on the garment. Fuse in place with the iron. (Photo 6)

Photo 1 – Tracing the design onto fusible web using a template.

Photo 2 – Cutting out the design.

Photo 3 – Fusing the web to the fabric.

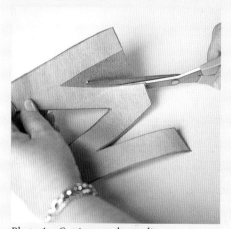
Photo 4 – Cutting out the appliqué.

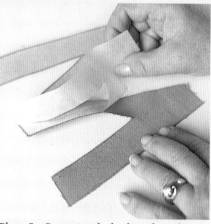
Photo 5 – Removing the backing from the appliqué.

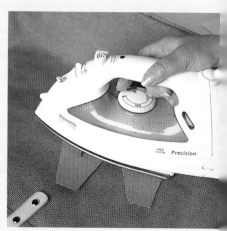
Photo 6 – Attaching the applique to the garment.

Circle Skirt

See page 36 for instructions.

Circle Skirt

Pictured on page 35

SUPPLIES

Base:

Linen skirt

Embellishments:

1/2 yd. cotton fabric in *each* color – Khaki green, salmon, plum, blue, brown

Embroidery floss to match fabric

Tools & Other Supplies:

Embroidery needle

Light fusible web

Tracing paper

Transfer paper and stylus

Scissors

INSTRUCTIONS

1. Trace the circle patterns and transfer 10 of each size to the paper side of the iron-on adhesive. Cut out.
2. Fuse circles on the wrong sides of the various colors of fabric, placing the circles at least 1/2" apart.
3. Cut out the fabric circles 1/8" larger all around than the paper backing to allow fraying.
4. Position large circles around the bottom of the skirt. Fuse in position.
5. Center the medium circles on the large circles and fuse in place. See Fig. 1 for color arrangements.
6. Center the small circles on the medium circles and iron in place. See the diagram for color arrangements.

Brightly colored circles of fabric are layered and stitched onto a neutral linen skirt for an updated contemporary look. The more the garment is washed the better the circles look as they fray and become worn looking. Pair this skirt with *The Easiest Tee,* which has the same running stitch embroidery. See page 76 for instructions.

by Patty Cox

7. Embellish with running stitches. Thread an embroidery needle with all six strands of one color of embroidery floss. Sew a running stitch (Fig. 2.) 1/8" from each circle edge using a contrasting floss color. Knot the floss on the inside of the skirt. ○

Fig. 1
Color arrangement of circles

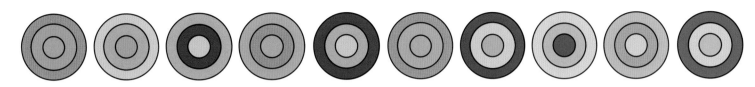

Fig. 2
Running Stitch

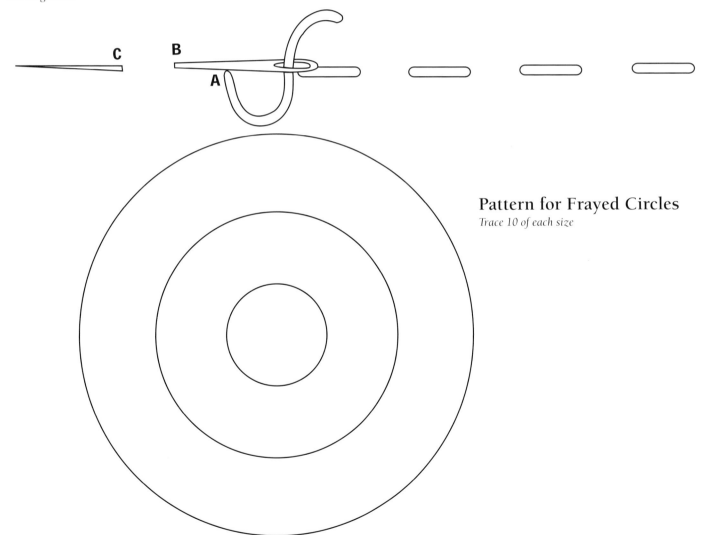

Pattern for Frayed Circles
Trace 10 of each size

Dress in Bloom

SUPPLIES

Base: Linen dress

Embellishments:
1/4 yd. green cotton or linen fabric
1/4 yd. salmon cotton fabric

Tools & Other Supplies:
Thread to match fabrics
Light fusible web
Sewing needle
Scissors
Sewing machine
Iron
Optional: Fabric glue

INSTRUCTIONS

Apply the Leaves:

1. Using the patterns provided, draw 14 large and 22 small leaves on the paper side of the fusible web.
2. Cut out the leaves from the fusible web.
3. Following the adhesive manufacturer's instructions, iron the leaves on the wrong side of the green fabric, placing them at least 1/2" apart.
4. Cut out the fabric leaves, making them 1/8" larger all around the paper backing to allow fraying.
5. Position the leaves around the dress neckline and bottom hem, using the placement diagrams (Figs. 1 and 2) as guides. Iron in position.
6. Machine straight stitch the leaves 1/8" from the edges.

Make the Yo-Yo Flowers:

1. Using the pattern provided, cut 13 circles from salmon fabric, each 2$\frac{1}{4}$" in diameter.
2. Turn under raw edges 1/8"and press to hold.
3. Working one circle at a time, use a needle and matching thread to hand gather each circle along the turned edge. (You're tacking down the edge at the same time.)
4. Pull gathers tight. Knot and cut thread. Repeat for remaining circles.
5. Position yo-yos on and around the leaves, using Figs. 1 and 2 as guides for placement. Sew or glue in place. ○

Fabric appliqué leaves and tiny hand-sewn yo-yos create colorful borders around the neckline and hem of a simple linen dress. We love the frayed edges of the leaves. Patterns and placement diagrams appear on page 40.

by Patty Cox

Neckline

Hemline

Dress in Bloom

See page 38 for instructions.

Patterns

Yo-yo

Cut 13 from salmon fabric

Large leaf

Cut 14 from green fabric

Small leaf

Cut 22 from green fabric

*Fig. 2 –
Placement diagram
for bottom hem*

Tropical Denim Jacket

See page 42 for instructions.

Patterns

Enlarge 200% for actual size

Tropical Denim Jacket

SUPPLIES

Base:

Denim jacket

Embellishments:

1/4 yd. *each* cotton fabric – Blue, red, yellow, lime green, green

Thread to match fabrics

4 yds. strung red sequins

Red seed beads

Tools & Other Supplies:

Light fusible web

Jewel glue

Iron

Sewing machine

Transfer paper and stylus

A colorful parrot perches among tropical leaves on the back of a denim jacket. Red sequins and red seed beads provide sparkle. The patterns appear on page 41.

by Patty Cox

INSTRUCTIONS

Apply Appliques:

1. Following the manufacturer's instructions, iron the fusible adhesive to the wrong sides of the fabrics.
2. Enlarge the patterns provided as directed. Transfer to the appropriate color fabrics. Cut out fabric appliques.

Option: Flip pattern pieces. Transfer to paper side of fusible adhesive. Iron adhesive side to the appropriate fabric. Cut out fabrics on penciled lines.

3. Assemble fabric pieces on jacket back. Iron in position.
4. Sew a fine satin stitch around each fabric piece, using matching thread.

Add Sequin Trim:

1. Squeeze a narrow line of jewel glue along the bottom edge of the jacket. Position red sequins on glue. Let dry. Secure each end with a small stitch, using a needle and red thread.
2. Glue sequins along the edge of each cuff. Let dry. Secure sequin ends.
3. Position and glue individual sequins around the appliqued design. Let dry.
4. Secure the sequins by sewing a seed bead in the center of each one, using a needle and red thread. ❍

Fresh as a Daisy Jacket

SUPPLIES

Base:

Denim Jacket

Embellishments:

White silk daisy

Lime green metallic ribbon

Turquoise metallic rick rack

1 pkg. round jewels with flat backs, assorted colors and sizes

Fabric scraps – assorted colors (2 flower colors, 2 flower center colors, 2 leaf colors)

Tools & Other Supplies:

Permanent jewel glue

6-strand embroidery floss, assorted colors

Embroidery needle

Scissors

Tracing paper

Pencil

Transfer paper and stylus

INSTRUCTIONS

1. Using the patterns provided, trace them onto tracing paper, and then transfer patterns to fabric. Cut out two daisy flower petal pieces and two flower centers and six leaves (reverse the pattern to cut three of the leaves.

2. Pin the flower petal pieces to the jacket, using the photo as a guide. Add a flower center piece on top of each petal piece.

3. Using two strands of embroidery floss, stitch the flowers centers to the jacket through the petals with straight running stitches approximately 1/8" from the edge.

4. Pin one end of the green ribbon under each flower petal piece and stitch the flower petals to the jacket, securing the ribbons under the flowers.

5. Pin the ribbon to the jacket in random curves to make the flower stems. Fold the cut ends at the bottom edge of the jacket back under the ribbon and pin.

6. Stitch the ribbon to the jacket with a tacking stitch every 1/4", using thread or floss in a coordinating color.

7. Pin the leaves to the stems. Stitch each leaf with a running stitch, using two strands of embroidery floss.

8. Position the white silk daisy on the pocket. Cut two 6" pieces of rick rack and fold each piece in half to make loops. Pin the ends under the silk daisy so that the loops are to the top right of the daisy.

9. Remove the daisy and glue the rick rack ends to the jacket. Glue the silk daisy to the jacket over the ends of the rick rack. Let dry.

10. Lay the jacket flat and position the assorted jewels on the jacket, using the photo as a guide for placement. The jewels along the center front are approximately 1" apart; the other jewels are placed randomly on the jacket front. Using jewel glue, glue each jewel to the jacket. Allow to dry undisturbed. ○

A silk flower provides a three-dimensional accent on this appliqued jeans jacket. Metallic ribbon creates the sparkling curved stems.

by Phyllis Dobbs

Patterns

Daisy & Leaf
Enlarge 122% for Actual Size

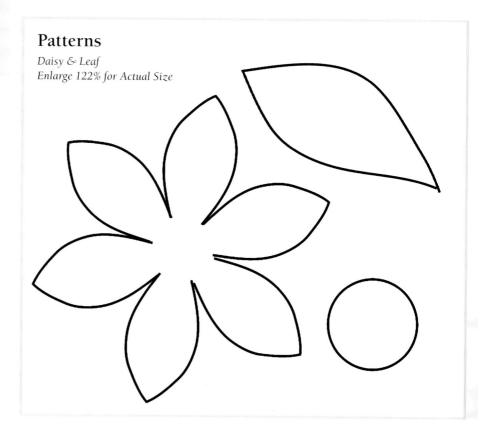

Tropical Leaves Tee

SUPPLIES

Base:

Sleeveless t-shirt

Embellishments:

Dimensional fabric paint – Peridot
    pearl, blue glitter, crystal glitter

1/4 yd. green fabric (for appliques)

6 round flat-backed jewels, 8mm – Blue

4 teardrop flat-backed jewels, 20mm
    long – 2 blue, 2 crystal

Tools & Other Supplies:

Fusible web

Scissors

Pencil

Iron

Here is a *no-sew* technique for fabric applique. The tropical leaves were attached to the garment with fusible web, then outlined with dimensional fabric paint. The technique is quick and fun to do, adds glitter and shine, and is durable.

INSTRUCTIONS

1. Using the pattern provided, trace three leaves onto the paper side of the fusible web.
2. Cut out the leaves.
3. Fuse leaves to the wrong side of the green fabric. Allow to cool.
4. Cut out fabric leaves, allowing a slight margin of fabric around the paper.
5. Following the fusible web manufacturer's instructions, fuse the fabric leaf appliques in position around the neckline of the garment. Use the photo as a guide for placement.
6. Outline and add veins and tendrils to the leaves with peridot pearl dimensional fabric paint.
7. Place a variety of dots on the leaves to resemble dewdrops using crystal glitter fabric paint. (They'll have the look of sequins.)
8. Attach the gems to the garment using blue glitter dimensional paint. See the photo for placement
9. Using blue glitter paint, make dots of paint – these are like beads – along the neckline of the garment. Allow to dry undisturbed overnight. ◯

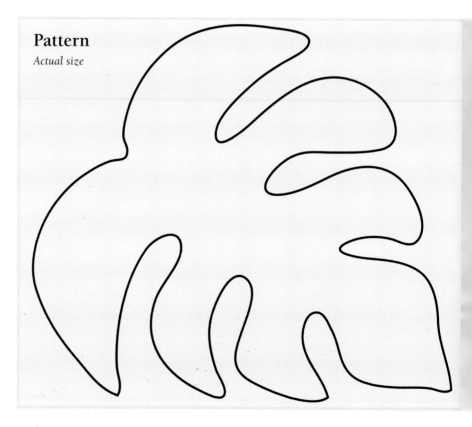

Pattern
Actual size

Personal Statement Tote

SUPPLIES

Base:

Orange burlap tote

Embellishments:

1/4 yd. green cotton fabric (for appliques)

Scrap of dark purple cotton fabric (for appliqués)

Melon-colored embroidery floss

Tools & Other Supplies:

Embroidery needle

Fusible web

Scissors

Pencil

Iron

Tracing paper

Transfer paper

INSTRUCTIONS

1. Find an alphabet on your computer or from clip art that you would like to use for your monograms. Enlarge to the size needed for your tote. Print out letters needed.

This simple burlap tote was a great color, but a little plain. It was quickly stylized and personalized with the addition of a monogram and an olive branch peace symbol. The fabric appliqués were first fused to the bag with fusible web and then embroidery floss was used to do a simple whip stitch around the perimeter of the pieces.

The olive branch has been a symbol of peace and prosperity since Ancient Greece. Later, in Ancient Rome, defeated soldiers carried olive branch in order to seek peace. The olive branch continues today to be a symbol for peace in the United States and Europe. We can see the olive branch on the United States' Great Seal where the eagle grasps a branch in his right talon as well as in the seal of the United Nations.

2. Cut out letters to use as a template. Place template letters on the paper side of the fusible web and trace around them. (*Be sure to reverse letters when tracing around them.*) Cut out the letters from the fusible web.

3. Fuse the letters to the wrong side of the green fabric. Cut out fabric letters.

4. Remove paper backing from the letter and fuse the fabric letters to the tote.

5. Use all the strands of the embroidery floss to whip stitch around the letters.

6. Trace the leaf, branch and olive patterns onto tracing paper. Transfer these patterns using transfer paper onto the paper side of the fusible web. (Reverse the branch pattern.) You will need seven leaves. Cut roughly around the patterns.

7. Fuse the leaf patterns to the back side of the green fabric and the branch and olive patterns to the purple fabric. Cut out appliqué pieces on pattern lines.

8. Remove the paper backing and fuse the appliqué pieces to the tote. Use the photo as a guide for placement. ◯

Pattern

Enlarge to 135% for actual size

Chapter 3

Embellishing with Iron-on Motifs

Iron-ons you can buy at fabric or craft departments include embroidered motifs with a hand-sewn look, stud and rhinestone iron-ons that provide three-dimensional metallic and jewel accents, flocked iron-on appliques that have a velvety texture, and color transfer iron-ons with a handpainted look and feel. They are a quick, easy way to add color and texture to simple garments and accessories. After heat is applied, the transfer is permanently sealed to the fabric.

General Information

How to Apply

- Read all instructions before beginning.
- Prewash fabric; do not use fabric softener.
- Do not use steam; remove water from the iron. Always test the heated iron on an inconspicuous area to avoid scorching.
- Be careful not to iron fronts of clothing to backs of clothing. TIP: Use a cardboard insert between clothing layers.
- Motifs with studs and stones work best on flat fabric, not seams.

For studs and rhinestones:

1. Remove white backing from design and place adhesive side on fabric, leaving clear sticky film in place.
2. Using a hard, flat surface such as a wooden cutting board, iron on a cotton setting for 30 to 60 seconds. Heavier fabrics may require more time, lighter fabrics, less time. Apply pressure on top of design. Do not move side to side or rock iron – this may cause studs or stones to shift. Allow to cool.
3. Slowly remove the clear sticky film, making sure all pieces of the motif have adhered to the fabric. **Do not** touch the studs-they will be very hot! If all pieces did NOT adhere, place film back on fabric and reapply heat for an additional 20 to 30 seconds. If top plastic has shrunk, apply studs directly to garment and iron. Allow to cool.
4. Turn garment inside out and apply heat to back of design area for about 30 seconds.

For embroidered iron-on motifs:

1. Gently remove design from backing card. (Photo 1.)

2. Position the design and place in desired area with adhesive side on the fabric. When placing motifs, the adhesive backing allows you to move the motifs around until you determine the exact placement before ironing. (Photo 2)
3. Using a hard, flat surface such as a wooden cutting board as a base, iron on design using a cotton setting. Press and hold for 30 to 60 seconds. Heavier fabrics may require more time, lighter fabrics, less time. (Photo 3)

4. Check to see if all the parts of the motif are securely adhered. If they are not, reapply heat for an additional 20 to 30 seconds. Allow to cool.
5. Turn garment inside out and apply heat to back of design area for about 20 seconds.

CARE

Turn garment inside out before washing. Hand wash, line dry.

Photo 1

Photo 2

Photo 3

Finished

Metallic Flowers on Linen

SUPPLIES

Base:

Linen pants

Embellishments:

Silver flower iron-on applique

Silver iron-on studs

1½ yds. ribbon with silver polka dots, 7/16" wide

Tool & Other Supplies:

Thread to match ribbon

Measuring tape

Chalk pencil

Pins

Cardboard

Iron

Scissors

Sewing machine *or* sewing needle

Silver floral appliques, silver studs, and silver-dotted ribbon provide metallic accents to a pair of linen pants. The appliqués are placed randomly and widely apart to give just a hint of glitz.

by Miche Baskett

INSTRUCTIONS

1. Measure 3½" up from the bottom of each pants leg and mark with chalk all the way around to make a guideline for sewing the ribbon.

2. Using the chalk marks as guides, position the ribbon around one pants leg with the ends of the ribbon meeting at the inside seam. Pin in place. Do the same for the other pants leg.

3. Using matching thread, sew the ribbon around the pant leg. Be careful not to sew the pant leg together, and remove the pins as you come to them.

4. Position the iron-on flowers on the pants, using the project photo as a guide for placement. Following the manufacturer's instructions, adhere the appliques to the pants. Save the backing papers from the appliques.

5. Arrange the iron-on studs over the flowers, using the photo as a guide. Place the saved backing paper over the flowers to protect them from the iron as you follow the manufacturer's instructions for adhering the studs to the pants. ○

Studded Tank

A V-neck tank-style tee looks anything but ordinary when decorated with iron-studs and rhinestones. Iron-on studs are easy to use on knits and more comfortable to wear than studs with prongs.

by Miche Baskett

SUPPLIES

Base:

Tank top

Embellishments:

2 pkgs. iron-on appliques – studs and rhinestones flower

Tools & Other Supplies:

Cardboard

Iron

Scissors

INSTRUCTIONS

Use the photo as a guide for placement and follow the manufacturer's instructions for adhering the iron-on studs to the shirt. ○

Koi Tote

SUPPLIES

Base:
Canvas tote, 13½" square

Embellishments:
Koi iron-on painted-look applique

Brown linen fabric, 9½" square

1¼ yds. orange ribbon, 5/8" wide

Rhinestones, 1/2" – 4 gold, 1 blue,

Rhinestones, 1/4" – 8 gold, 7 blue,
   5 red oval

Rhinestones. 3/16" – 6 blue, 2 red,
   6 green

Tools & Other Supplies:
Jewel glue

Fabric glue

Ruler

Cardboard

Iron

Scissors

INSTRUCTIONS

1. Position the koi applique in the center of the linen fabric square. Following the manufacturer's instructions, adhere the iron-on applique to the fabric.

2. Embellish the applique with rhinestones, using jewel glue to attaching them and the project photo as a guide. Reserve four 1/2" gold rhinestones and eight 1/4" gold rhinestones for the ribbon frame.

3. Place the decorated linen fabric square on the front of the tote bag. Use a ruler to make sure it is centered. Adhere with fabric glue.

4. Test fabric glue on a small section of the ribbon to make sure it will not show through. Allow to dry. Continue if the test results are satisfactory. (If your ribbon is too shear and the fabric glue show through, it might be necessary for you to sew the ribbon to the tote.)

5. Cut pieces of ribbon to fit the edges of the fabric square. Position the ribbon pieces around the fabric to form a frame, folding under the cut ends. Glue in place with fabric glue.

6. Embellish the corners of the ribbon frame with the reserved gold rhinestones, using jewel glue to attach. See the photo for placement. ◯

Here's a no-sew solution to the plain canvas tote. An iron-on applique is placed on a fabric panel, framed with ribbon, and embellished with colorful stones. It's a designer look at a fraction of the cost.

by Miche Baskett

Embroidered Vines Linen Pants

SUPPLIES

Base:

Linen pants

Embellishments:

6 pkgs. iron-on appliques –
   embroidered vine

Tools & Other Supplies:

Thread to match pants

Measuring tape

Cardboard

Iron

Scissors

Sewing machine *or* sewing needle

Call attention to your beautiful legs with these embroidered vine appliques that frame the side slits of a pair of linen pants. This is a great way
to restyle a pair of pants that are not quite the right length.

by Miche Baskett

INSTRUCTIONS

1. Cut about $5^{1}/_{4}$" up both sides of the
   outside seam of each pants leg. (Fig. 1)
2. Turn pants inside out. Fold under the
   cut edges of the openings 1/4". Press.
   Turn under another 1/4". Press.
3. Using matching thread, hem the edges
   of the slits. Turn pants right side out.

4. Arrange the iron-on vine appliques
   along the slits on the pants legs,
   using the photo as a guide for placement. Following the manufacturer's
   instructions, adhere the applique to
   the pants. ○

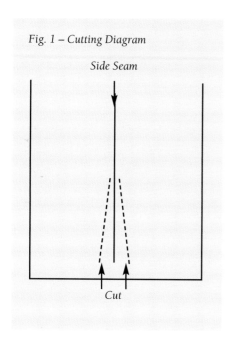

Fig. 1 – Cutting Diagram

Side Seam

Cut

Sheer Glitz Tank Top

SUPPLIES

Base:

Tank top

Embellishments:

1 yd. sheer fabric

10 pkgs. appliques – rhinestone vine

55 hot-fix rhinestones, 3/16"

Tools & Other Supplies:

Thread to match top

Chalk pencil

Measuring tape

Yardstick

Sewing needle

Straight pins

Cardboard

Iron

Scissors

Hot fix applicator tool

Optional: Sewing machine, non-stick paper such as wax paper

A sheer fabric insert on the back of a tank top is embellished with iron-on rhinestone vines, and a line of rhinestones is placed along the top edge of the insert. You can do the sewing by hand or use a sewing machine to attach the insert to the garment.

by Miche Baskett

INSTRUCTIONS

Add the Insert:

1. Turn the tank top inside out. Use the measuring tape to measure, then mark a line with chalk down the center back of the tank.
2. Measure and mark the center line about 10" from the top.
3. Use the yardstick to draw straight lines from the tops of the shoulder seams to the 10" mark on the center line. (See Fig. 1)
4. Cut along the lines to make a deep V-shaped cutout down the back of the tank.
5. Fold the cut edges back 1/4" and press in place.
6. Place the sheer fabric over the cutout area and mark an area big enough to cover the entire cutout plus 1/2" on both sides. Mark a V-shape along the neckline edge of the sheer fabric.
7. Cut out the marked area of the sheer fabric.
8. Fold under the cut edges and the neckline of the sheer fabric piece. Fold inward about 1/4", then fold inward again 1/4" to hem. Press the folds. Sew the hem along the neckline and side edges.
9. With the top right side out, place the sheer fabric under the V-shaped cutout in the top and pin in place.
10. Sew the sheer fabric to the tank, stitching along the folded and pressed cut edges of the tank.

Embellish the Tank

1. Place a piece of cardboard inside the tank to keep it stiff and in place.
2. Arrange the iron-on vines on the tank, allowing some of the vines to overlap the area where the two fabrics meet. Cut some of the iron-on shapes to suit your design, using the photo as a guide. When arranging the iron-ons, save the backing paper.
3. Follow the embellishment manufacturer's instructions for adhering the rhinestone vines. **Important:** Take special care because you are working with sheer fabric. Place the backing paper from the rhinestone vines or other non-stick paper under each area as you iron it. (If you don't, the glue from the iron-ons will go through the sheer fabric and stick to the cardboard. TIP: Test your procedure on a scrap piece of sheer fabric before working with your garment.
4. Attach rhinestones along the top of the sheer insert, covering the hem. ◯

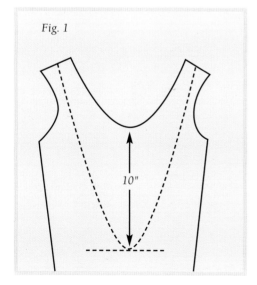

Fig. 1

10"

Flower Garland Dress

SUPPLIES

Base:

Black tank dress

Embellishments:

3 pkgs. iron-on appliques –
  embroidered flowers

Tools & Other Supplies:

Cardboard

Iron

Small, very sharp scissors

INSTRUCTIONS

1. Position the appliques close together around the neckline of the dress, arranging them so the first row starts just below the hem of the neckline. It's okay to overlap the appliques; use the photo as a guide or create your own arrangement.
2. Following the applique manufacturer's instructions, iron on the appliques to adhere them to the dress.
3. Use sharp scissors to cut away the dress fabric along the top edge of the appliques so that the neckline takes the shape of the flower design. ○

Colorful embroidered flowers make a glorious garland when arranged around the neckline of a simple black dress. The dress neckline is cut along the shape of the embroidered flowers to create a scalloped neckline.

by Miche Baskett

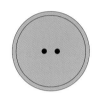

Chapter 4

Embellishing with Paint

Fabric paint is a fun medium to use for decorating your garments, and it allows for some creative options. Acrylic paint that has been especially developed for painting on fabric makes decorating your garments easy. There are a variety of brands available in a wide range of color options, including metallic, glitter, pearl, and glossy colors. For best results, use paint that is especially developed for painting on fabric, and always follow the manufacturer's instructions and recommendations for the brand of paint you are using.

Beaded Tee
See page 66 for instructions.

General Supplies & Instructions

Fabric Paint

Brush-on fabric paints are liquid paints that are absorbed into the fabric and maintain a soft feel. They have a durable, flat sheen when dry. These acrylic paints are water-based and non-toxic. They can be applied with brushes or sponge tools and are suitable for stenciling. *Note:* If you can't find "fabric paint," use acrylic craft paint mixed with a textile medium.

Dimensional fabric paints are used straight from the bottle. Usually the bottle has a nozzle or writer tip for making single lines or perfect dots. Use dimensional paint for lettering, making curlicues, outlining, adding dots, or adhering jewels and crystals to fabric. **Do not** mix dimensional paints with water. TIP: Wipe off the tip of the bottle before replacing the cap. Paint build-up will cause the tip of the bottle to bend, resulting in poor outlines.

Tools

When using brush-on fabric paints, you will need **artist brushes, sponges, or stencil brushes.** Brushes made especially for painting on fabric make the job a little easier – they have stiffer bristles that allow the paint to be almost *scrubbed* into the fabric. The round sponge-on-a-stick tool shown has a flat bottom – use it to sponge dots on a garment or to apply paint through a stencil. You can find these types of brushes in craft or art supply stores where acrylic paints or stencil paints are sold. Squeeze puddles of paint on a **palette** to load your brushes. Use a purchased palette or a foam throw-away plate or tray. Designs can be easily stenciled onto your garment using **stencils** and a **stencil brush.**

Preparing Fabric Items

Before painting on fabric, wash and iron it following the temperature recommendations for the fabric type you are using. **Do not** use fabric softener or dryer sheets as these products can prevent paints from adhering properly.

Protecting Fabric

I like to enclose the fabric in plastic and expose the design area only to protect the item from any paint smudges or accidents. This technique leaves only the design accessible and the rest of the fabric area protected. To keep the paint from seeping onto areas where you don't want it, cover a piece of cardboard with wax paper and place the cardboard behind the area of the fabric you are painting.

Here's how:

1. Cut a piece of cardboard that is a little larger than the design pattern.
2. Tape or pin the fabric to the cardboard. NOTE: Some people like to use a piece of freezer paper under the fabric so paint won't seep onto the cardboard. I do not, but you can do this if you want to protect the cardboard.
3. Slip the whole thing – the garment and the cardboard – into a plastic bag.
4. Carefully cut away the plastic bag over the areas where you are going to paint.
5. Tape down the raw edges of the plastic with masking tape.

Undercoating

If you are applying light colors of paint on a dark piece of fabric, you will need to undercoat the design area with white paint. Undercoating ensures better coverage and true colors. To undercoat, transfer the design and paint the design area with white paint. Let dry. A second coat may be needed for even coverage. When the undercoating is thoroughly dry, paint the design, covering the white area.

Drying & Curing

The following instructions are for typical fabric paints on the market. *Always follow the manufacturer's instructions and recommendations for the brand of paint you are using.* Heat setting is recommended for best durability.

- **Air drying.** Allow paints to air dry for 24 hours before wearing. The paint will be completely cured in 72 hours and then can be washed.
- **Heat setting in a clothes dryer.** Allow the painted design to dry overnight. Place the item in a clothes dryer for 30 minutes on the highest setting allowed for the type of fabric.
- **Heat setting with an iron.** Allow the painted design to dry overnight, then heat set using a dry iron and a pressing cloth. Heat the iron to the highest setting allowed for the fabric you are using. Lay the pressing cloth over the painted fabric. Place the iron on the painted area for 10 seconds, then lift the iron and move it to another area. **Do not** slide the iron across the fabric. **Do not iron over dimensional paint.** For more delicate fabrics, shorten the heating time.

Fabric Care

Wash fabrics painted with fabric paints by hand or in a washing machine using cool water and line dry rather than placing in a clothes dryer. Areas painted with *brush-on paints* can be ironed. **Do not** iron over *dimensional paints.* **Do not** dry clean.

Using Brush-on Fabric Paint

Liquid fabric paints may be brushed, sponged, or stenciled on. Use fabric paint just as you would any acrylic paint. Squeeze puddles of paint onto your palette to make brush loading easier. Fabric absorbs paint; therefore, use plenty of paint on your brush. When painting with fabric paints, **do not** thin paints with water – it will interfere with the performance of the paint. Brush-on colors can be inter-mixed, and paint can be layered for shading and highlighting. If mishaps occur, clean up immediately while the paint is wet with soap and water.

Making Dots with a Sponge Tool

Round sponge-on-a-stick tools (some-times called "spouncers") can be loaded with either brush-on or dimensional paint, then "pounced" on the garment to create perfect dots of color. These sponge tools can be found in a variety of sizes.

1. Squeeze a puddle of paint on a palette. (Photo 1)
2. Fill the sponge tool with paint by dabbing into the paint puddle. (Photo 2). Dab the sponge up and down on a clean place on the palette to make sure the sponge is filled evenly with paint.
3. Pounce or dot the sponge onto the fabric. It is as easy as that to make perfect polka dots. (Photo 3).

Photo 1 – Squeezing a puddle of paint on palette.

Photo 2 – Loading a sponge tool with paint.

Photo 3 – Pouncing paint on fabric to make a dot.

Using Dimensional Paints

Use dimensional paint colors straight from the bottle, placing the applicator tip of the bottle on the fabric. Allow to dry before moving the fabric.

Making Dots or Lines with Dimensional Paint

To make a dot of paint, touch the writer tip of a bottle of dimensional paint to the fabric surface. Gently squeeze out the amount of paint needed for the size dot desired. Lift tip. (Photo 4)

When making a line of paint, touch the bottle tip to the surface and squeeze. Pull the tip along, holding it just slightly above the fabric surface. Touch

Photo 4 – Making a dot.

the tip down on fabric and stop squeez-ing to end the line. (Photo 5)

When outlining, hold the bottle at an angle and move the bottle around the

Photo 5 – Making a line.

design, pulling it toward you. Keep your hand steady and use smooth move-ments. For thinner lines, move the bot-tle more quickly. Avoid pushing the bottle into the paint.

Beaded Tees

Dimensional fabric paint, applied here in patterns of dots and dashes, gives the look of beading around the necklines of two t-shirts. See the beginning of this chapter for information about using dimensional fabric paints. *TIP:* Practice on some scrap fabric to perfect your technique before you work on an actual garment. Always follow the paint manufacturer's instructions for applying and curing the paint and caring for the painted shirt.

by Miche Baskett

SUPPLIES

Base:

For the Green Shirt

Long-sleeved t-shirt with rounded neckline

For the Red Shirt

Long-sleeved V-neck t-shirt

Embellishments:

Dimensional fabric paints – Metallic copper (for the green shirt), fresh foliage (for the red shirt)

Tools & Other Supplies:

Ruler

Chalk pencil

INSTRUCTIONS

Use a ruler and a chalk pencil to draw guidelines around the neckline of your shirt. The designs are simply dots of paint made with the bottle nozzle tip interspersed with short straight lines. See the photos for examples. ○

Seeing Spots Tote

SUPPLIES

Base:

1/2 yd. black fabric

Black thread

2 red purse handles

Embellishments:

Dimensional fabric paint – Metallic peridot, pearl white, metallic pure gold, engine red

Tools & Other Supplies:

Chalk pencil

Ruler

Scissors

Safety pin

Sewing machine

Iron

Sewing needle

Circle templates, 3/4" to 2½"

Dots of dimensional paint, applied in circular patterns, are reminiscent of a holiday fireworks display. We've included instructions for making your own purse, but you could use the embellishing idea for a purchased cloth purse of any size.

by Miche Baskett

INSTRUCTIONS

Make the Purse

1. Cut two 12" squares of black fabric.
2. Place the pieces, right sides together, and sew around three sides.
3. Double fold the edges of the open end. Press. Hem the open end.
4. Measure the size of the slit in the purse handles. Cut a strip of black fabric a little more than double the width of the slit and 8" long.
5. Fold the strip of fabric in half with right sides together. Press. Sew along the long cut edge. Trim the seam.
6. Attach a safety pin to one end and pull the strip down into itself. Keep pulling until the strip is right side out. Press. Cut the strip in four equal pieces.
7. Measure and mark where you want to attach the handles.
8. Attach the handles with the fabric strips by putting a strip through the handle slit, turning under the raw edges, and hand sewing in place.
9. Turn the purse right side out.

Embellish:

1. Use a chalk pencil and the circle templates to draw circles of various sizes randomly on the front of the purse. Use the photo as a guide.
2. Practice making dots with dimensional paint on scrap fabric from the purse. Hold the bottle upright and squeeze to force paint through the applicator top, keeping the tip off the surface of the fabric.
3. Using the photo as a guide, decide on a plan for color placement. Begin painting, making the dots on the outer edges of the circles, then working inward. Let dry, cure, and heat set according the paint manufacturer's instructions. ○

Dotted Denim Dress

SUPPLIES

Base:

Denim dress

Embellishments:

Fabric brush-on paints – Wicker white, lavender, coastal blue, yellow citron

Tools & Other Supplies:

Round sponge-on-a-stick applicator

Container for paint

Cardboard

Scrap fabric

Iron

Dots in three pastel shades are randomly placed on the front of a denim dress. Using a round sponge-on-a-stick applicator makes it easy to create uniform circles. Undercoating the circles with white paint ensures the pastel colors will stand out against the dark background.

by Miche Baskett

INSTRUCTIONS

1. Place the cardboard inside the dress under the side where you intend to add the dots.
2. Pour wicker white fabric paint into a container. Load the sponge applicator with the white paint.
3. Practice making polka dots on scrap fabric by gently placing the sponge brush down on the fabric and lifting directly up. Proceed when you are satisfied with the results.
4. Make white polka dots all over one side of the front of the dress with the sponge tool. See the photo for placement ideas. Allow to dry.
5. With the three paint colors, make dots on top of the white dots using the sponging tool. Use the photo as a guide for color placement.
6. Follow the paint manufacturer's instructions for drying, heat setting, and garment care. ○

Chapter 5

Embellishing with Embroidery

The embroidery projects in this chapter use thread, yarn, and beads to create designs and motifs that are outlined or filled in solidly with stitchery. Whether done by hand or machine, embroidery is a way to add color, texture, and decoration to your clothes.

Thread Embroidery Stitches

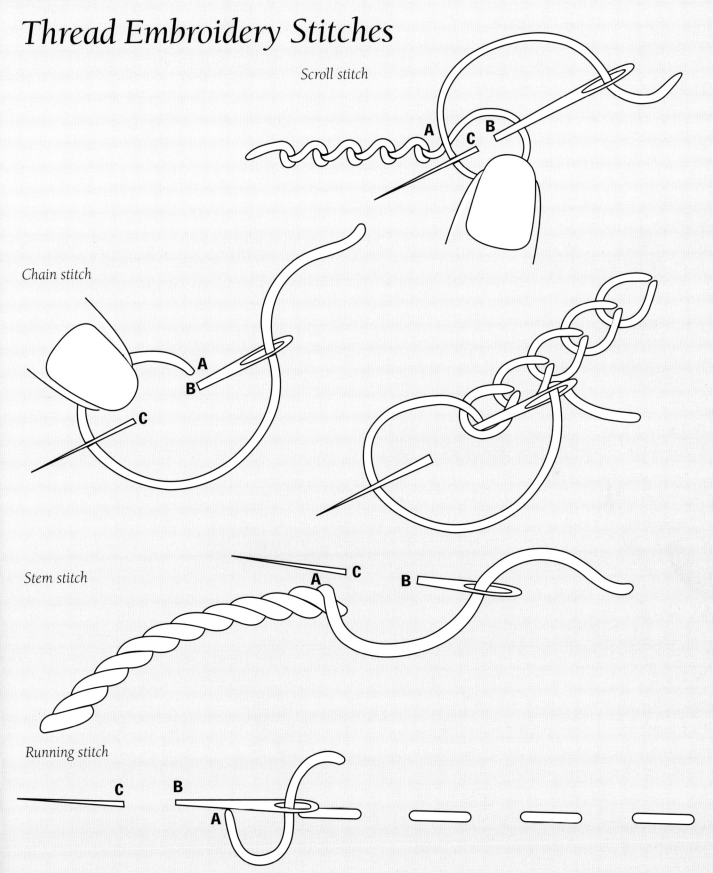

Scroll stitch

Chain stitch

Stem stitch

Running stitch

Beaded Embroidery Stitches

Single Stitch with Seed Beads

Bring up needle from back of fabric, through bead, and back down through fabric; pull thread snug to remove slack. Move needle at back of fabric to next bead position and repeat.

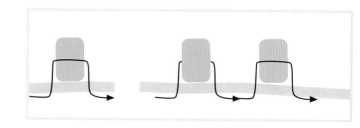

Backstitch

For a continuous row or line of beads.

First part: Bring up thread from back of fabric. Pick up 6 beads and go back into fabric near last bead, snugging the beads together. The beads should lay flat but close together and with no gaps or thread showing.

Second part: Bring needle back up between 4th and 5th stitched beads and go through the last two beads again, emerging from the last stitched bead.

Next stitch: Pick up 6 beads, go back into fabric near end bead, and come back up between 3rd and 2nd bead from stitched end. Go through last 2 stitched beads and pick up 6 more.

Repeat sequence to create a continuous row. TIP: Rows can be smoothed or straightened by running the needle and thread back through the entire row.

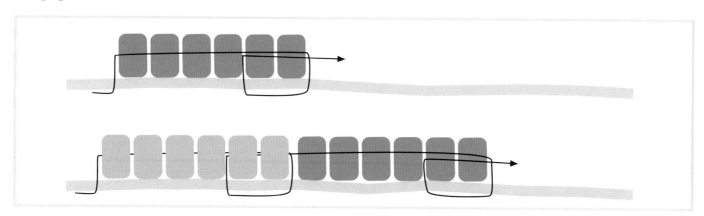

Bead Bridge

Bring up needle through fabric, pick up several seed beads and go back through fabric making a stitch shorter than the length of the beads, causing the beads to arch above surface of fabric. At back of fabric move needle to next position and repeat.

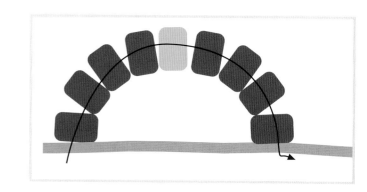

Backstitch with Bugle & Seed Beads

The thread rides on the seed beads so the sharp edges of the bugle beads won't wear or cut through.

First part: Bring up thread from back of fabric. Pick up one seed, one bugle, and one more seed. Go back into fabric near last bead.

Second part: Bring needle back up between bugle and last seed stitched and go through those two beads again, emerging from the last stitched seed.

Next stitch: Pick up another bugle and another seed and repeat the sequence.

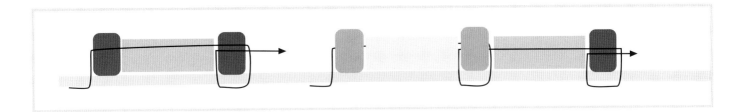

Bead Loop

Bring up needle through fabric at A, and pick up 8 beads. Take the needle back through the first bead and through fabric at B, forming a loop of beads. Repeat for next stitch.

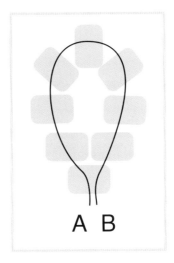

Bead Stack

Take needle through one or more beads, ending with a seed bead to serve as a Stop Bead that will hold the bead(s) below it in place. Take needle back through all except Stop Bead and through fabric. Pull thread snug to remove slack before proceeding to next bead.

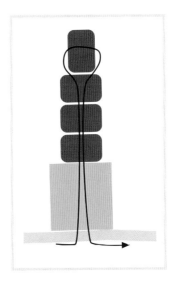

The Easiest Tee

SUPPLIES

Base:

Rust t-shirt

Embellishments:

3 colors embroidery floss

Tools & Other Supplies:

Large-eye embroidery needle

Wash-away fabric marker

INSTRUCTIONS

1. Measure and mark three rows 1/4"
   apart, starting at the neck edge, using
   a wash-away marker.
2. Thread the needle with all six strands
   of one color of embroidery floss.
   Knot the floss end. Sew a long running stitch (Fig. 1) 1/4" from neckline. Knot floss at the end of the row
   on the inside of the shirt.
3. Repeat with the remaining colors of
   floss to complete the other two rows.
   ○

Running stitches in three colors circle the neckline of this t-shirt. Nothing could be easier!

by Patty Cox

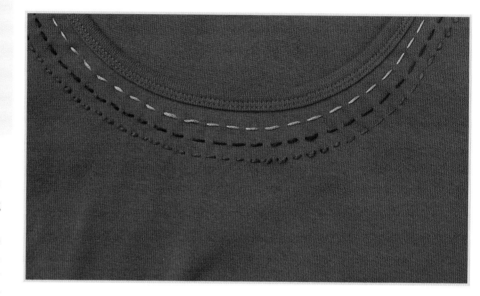

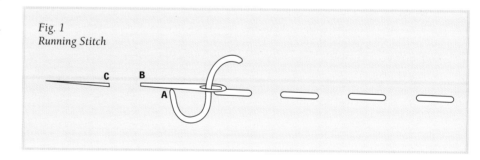

Fig. 1
Running Stitch

Sequins & Stitches Top

Four colors of embroidery floss and one bright line of shiny sequins decorate a turquoise tee. For diagrams of embroidery stitches, see page 73.

by Patty Cox

SUPPLIES

Base: Turquoise t-shirt

Embellishments:

Embroidery floss – Orange, pink, lime green, yellow gold

1/2 yd. fuchsia sequins

Tools & Other Supplies:

Large eye embroidery needle

Wash-away fabric marker

Fabric glue

INSTRUCTIONS

1. Measure and mark seven rows 1/2" apart around the neckline of the t-shirt, starting at the neck edge and using a wash-away marker.
2. Thread a needle with all six strands of pink embroidery floss. Knot floss end. Stem stitch top row. Knot floss at the end of the row on the inside of the shirt.
3. Chain stitch the second row, using six strands of orange embroidery floss.
4. Scroll stitch the third row, using six strands of yellow gold embroidery floss.
5. Stem stitch the fourth row, using six strands of lime green embroidery floss.
6. Squeeze a narrow line of fabric glue along the line of the fifth row. Place fuchsia sequins on glue. Allow to dry. Secure sequins with needle and pink thread.
7. Stem stitch the sixth row, using six strands of orange embroidery floss.
8. Scroll stitch the seventh row, using six strands of yellow gold embroidery floss. ○

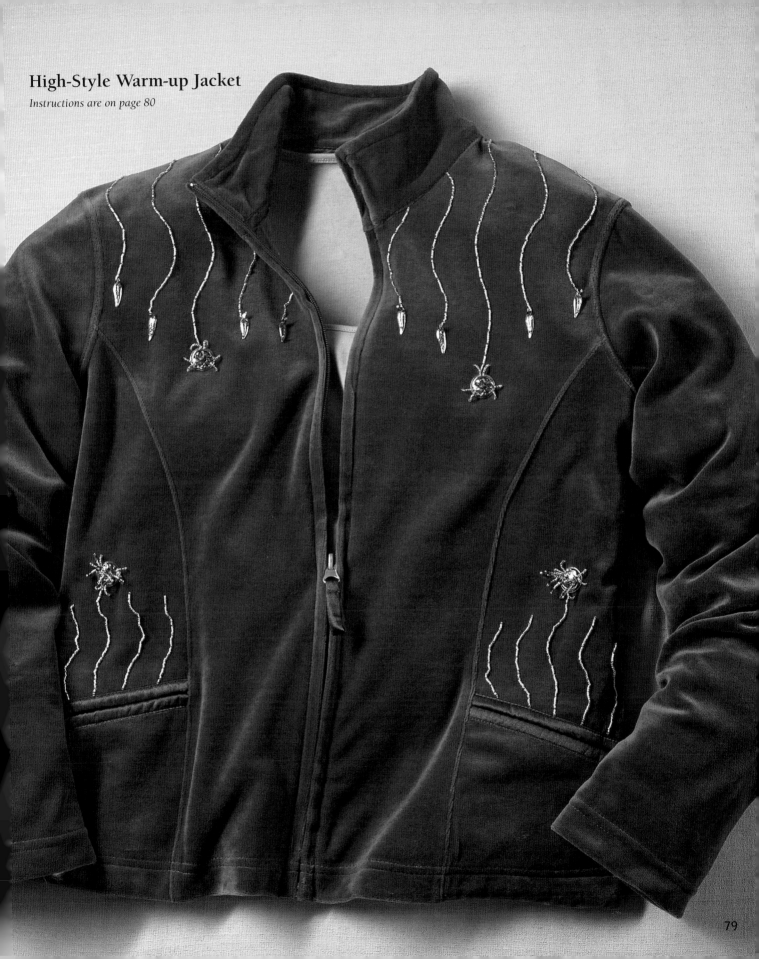

High-Style Warm-up Jacket

Instructions are on page 80

High-Style Warm-up Jacket

SUPPLIES

Base:

Cardigan style jacket, medium to
  heavyweight velour

Embellishments:

10 grams seed beads, size 11 –
  Silver-lined chartreuse

1 gram seed beads, size 15 –
  Silver-lined olivine

30 bicone crystals, 4mm – Montana
  Aurora Borealis

8 sterling silver small leaf beadable
  embellishments

4 sterling silver dome beadable
  embellishments

Tools & Other Supplies:

Beading thread – White, silver

Beading needle

Pencil

Tracing paper (for pattern transfer)

Tiny crochet hook *or* blunt-end needle

Before

A velvety casual jacket can be simply embellished to make it suitable for the dressiest occasion. The leaf and dome embellishments have holes to accommodate beaded enhancements. They are sterling silver, which will hold up to normal laundering, but should not be dry cleaned.

by Cindy Gorder

Pictured on page 79

INSTRUCTIONS

See the beginning of this chapter for diagrams and instructions for making beaded embroidery stitches.

Prepare & Embellish:

1. Trace or photocopy the pattern lines for the neck/shoulder area of the jacket. Make a mirror image of the pattern for the other side of the jacket front.
2. Position the pattern on one side of the jacket and carefully trim the pattern to fit the neck and shoulder area. Pin in place. (Photo 1) Do the same for the other side.
3. Carefully scribe the outermost pattern lines on one side using a tiny crochet hook or blunt-end needle into the nap of the velour. (Photo 2) **Note:** If you are using a different sort of fabric that won't allow the pattern to transfer in this manner, leave the pattern pinned in place and bead along the paper edges.

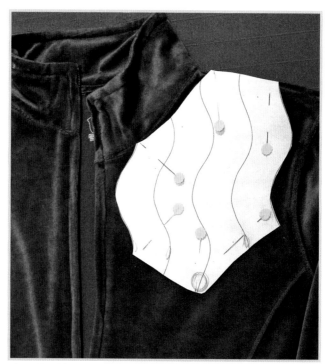

Photo 1 – After trimming to fit the neckline, the pattern is pinned in place.

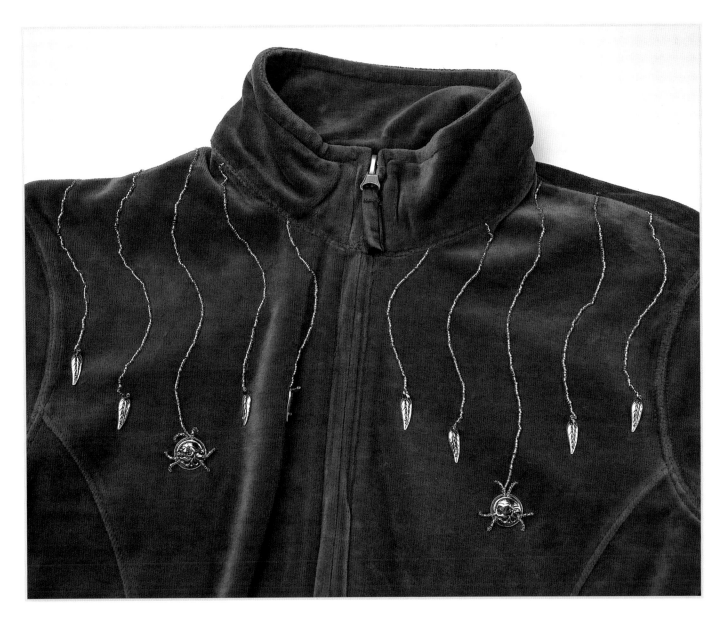

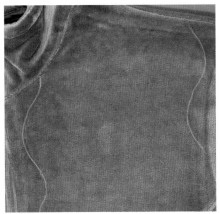

Photo 2 – The outermost pattern lines are scribed on the velour fabric.

4. Using size 11 seed beads and white beading thread, backstitch bead the outer two pattern lines.

5. Cut away the outer pattern lines, transfer the next two lines, and bead them.

6. Cut away the pattern on one side of the center line, transfer the center line, and bead it.

7. Using the mirror image of the pattern, follow the same process to bead the neck/shoulder area on the other side.

8. Use the pocket pattern and the same procedures to bead lines on the pockets with size 11 seed beads.

9. Stitch silver domes and leaves at the ends of the beading lines at the neck/shoulder areas, using the photo as a guide for placement.

10. Stitch domes to longest lines of the beadwork on the pockets.

Continued on next page

High Style Warm-up Jacket

Continued from page 81

Embellish Leaves & Domes:
Use silver thread for these steps.

1. Using size 15 seed beads, stitch 10-bead bridges radiating from the holes on the edges of all the domes.

2. On the domes in the neck/shoulder areas, make a bead loop in the center hole using three size 11 seed beads, one crystal, and three more size 11 seed beads. Make bead stacks in the holes on either side of the center, using a size 11 seed bead, a crystal, and a size 15 seed bead for the stop bead.

3. Stitch a single size 15 seed bead in the tip hole of each silver leaf.

4. Stitch a bead stack consisting of a crystal and a size 15 stop bead in the top hole of each leaf.

5. On the domes on the pockets, in addition to the bridges radiating from edges, stitch multiple bead stacks of seed beads in the center hole from a single crystal in center to make mini tassels.

6. On either side of the centers, stitch the bead stack tassels from a single size 11 seed bead. Add a crystal bead and a size 15 stop bead at the ends of some of the tassels; leave some without crystals. ○

Pattern for Pocket area

Adjust to fit your garment

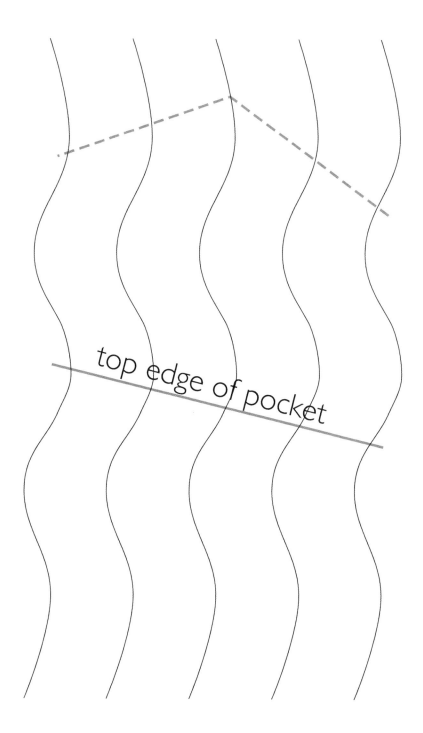

top edge of pocket

Pattern for Neck/Shoulder area

Adjust to fit your garment

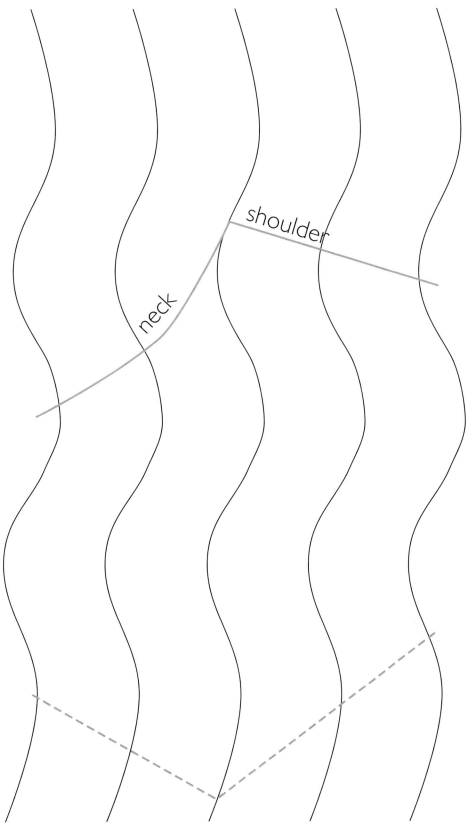

neck

shoulder

Beads & Denim Collar

SUPPLIES

Base:

Denim jacket

Embellishments:

1/4 yd. purple velveteen (or color of your choice)

1 tbsp. seed beads, size 8 – Pink lustre finish

2 tbsp. twisted bugles, size 5 – Pink iris finish

1 tbsp. seed beads, size 6 – Lavender opal gilt-lined

1/2 tsp. seed beads, size 15 – Lilac iris

1/2 tsp. seed beads, size 15 – Light champagne silver-lined

2 tbsp. seed beads, size 11 – Blue iris finish

1 tbsp. seed beads, size 11 – Teal blue silver-lined

2 moon face beads, 1/4" – Blue-green

Tools & Other Supplies:

Fusible interfacing

Beading thread – Purple *or* dark blue

Beading needle

Sewing needle

Permanent marker

Tiny crochet hook *or* blunt-end needle

A beaded velveteen collar turns a jeans jacket from ordinary to a chic one-of-a-kind fashion. Just this simple little touch makes a big statement. See the beginning of this chapter for diagrams and instructions for making beaded embroidery stitches.

by Cindy Gorder

INSTRUCTIONS

Prepare:

1. Lay jacket flat and pin fusible interfacing to collar. Trim interfacing 1/4" smaller than the collar on each end and the long outer edge. (Photo 1)
2. Trace or photocopy the pattern provided and enlarge to fit the collar of your jacket (See page 87).
3. Position the interfacing on the pattern, adhesive side down, matching at the centers. Adjust the pattern shape, if needed, to fit your collar. Trace the pattern onto the interfacing, using a permanent marker.
4. Fuse the interfacing to the wrong side of the velveteen. Cut out the velveteen 1/2" larger than the interfacing on all sides. (Photo 2)
5. Trace over the lines in the center of the pattern, using a tiny crochet hook or blunt-end needle. Turn over to see the pattern lines on the velveteen. Continue tracing pattern lines as you go; if you trace them all before you start, re-trace as needed, as handling the fabric may dull the lines. **Note: If** you're using a different type of fabric baste along the pattern lines with thread so you can see them on the front side of the fabric.

Continued on page 86

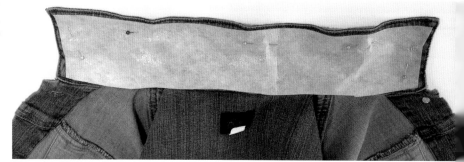

Photo 1 – *The interfacing is pinned to the collar.*

Photo 2 – *The interfacing (with the beading pattern drawn on it) is fused to the velveteen.*

Before

Beads & Denim

Continued from page 84

Bead:

1. Use alternating bugles and pink lustre seed beads to backstitch bead the rays of the central design.
2. Backstitch the arches using blue iris seed beads.
3. Backstitch the scroll designs on either side of the central motif using blue iris seed beads.
4. Backstitch the bead scrolls at the collar tips using teal blue seed beads.
5. Stitch two-bead stacks of pink lustre beads between the rays of the central motif. Turn the top (stop) bead on edge after the stitch is complete.
6. Stitch two-bead stacks of size 6 lavender and blue iris seed beads along the edges of the scrolls closest to the central motif.
7. Stitch two-bead stacks of pink lustre and champagne beads along the edges of the double scrolls (next from the center).
8. Single-stitch size 15 lilac beads along the edges of the remaining blue iris scrolls.
9. Stitch bugles bookended with blue iris seed beads randomly in the open areas of the design.
10. Stitch moon face beads at the ends of the scrolls at the collar tips.

Assemble:

1. Pin the beaded fabric to the jacket collar. Fold under the edges of the velveteen panel. Whipstitch the velveteen panel to denim collar along the edges, using a sewing needle.
2. Make a bead fringe along the short ends and long outer edge of the collar, using a bugle bead bookended with dark blue seed beads: Bring a threaded beading needle out from the edge of the fabric, pick up the three beads, and take needle back into same place on fabric. Move needle 1/4" away and repeat. ○

Pattern

Enlarge 200%.

Adjust as needed to fit your garment.

See page 84 for instructions.

De Colores Jacket

SUPPLIES

Base:

Black jacket

Embellishments:

Variegated polyester thread – Sunrise, ombre, pink ombre, turquoise ombre, neon lemon-lime

Metallic gold thread

Tools & Other Supplies:

Sewing machine capable of sewing a satin stitch with embroidery needle and metallic thread needle

Press-and-seal plastic wrap *or* fusible tearaway stabilizer

Light transfer paper and stylus

Seed beads and E beads in coordinating colors

Beading needle and thread

INSTRUCTIONS

For best results, use pieces of press-and-seal plastic wrap or tearaway stabilizer under the embroidery. See Fig. 1 for placement of motifs.

1. Remove the lining from the jacket. Open the sleeve seams.
2. Using the patterns given, transfer a leaf motif to the jacket. Cut a piece of press-and-seal plastic wrap just a bit larger than the leaf design. Adhere it on the inside of jacket under the transferred design.
3. Set the sewing machine on medium-width zig-zag with a very fine stitch. Satin stitch over the leaf outline with variegated thread.
4. Change thread colors. Satin stitch the inner leaf design.

Continued on page 90

Machine embroidered leaves and butterflies of bright and fanciful thread are splashed across the front and back of this black cotton jacket. Then the jacket is further embellished with machine stitching and beads to create the look of a vintage crazy quilt.

by Patty Cox

De Colores Jacket

Continued from page 88

5. Repeat steps 2, 3, and 4 to satin stitch all the leaves with variegated thread colors. Tear away the press-and-seal plastic wrap from the inside of the jacket.
   Option: Place press-and-seal plastic wrap over the leaf design and trace with a marker. Press the plastic wrap on the right side of the jacket. Satin stitch over the tracing. **Note:** There is more drag under the presser foot using this method.

6. Transfer the butterfly designs to the jacket.

7. Satin stitch the butterfly outlines with variegated thread.

8. Fill in each butterfly design with satin-stitched variegated thread.

9. Thread the machine with metallic thread. Set on zig-zag at 12 to 15 stitches per inch. Sew zig-zag lines around the embroidered motifs to create the crazy quilt pattern.

10. Hand sew seed beads and E beads on the jacket front around the embroidered designs.

11. Sew sleeve seams.

12. Replace jacket lining. ⭘

Fig. 1
Placement Diagram

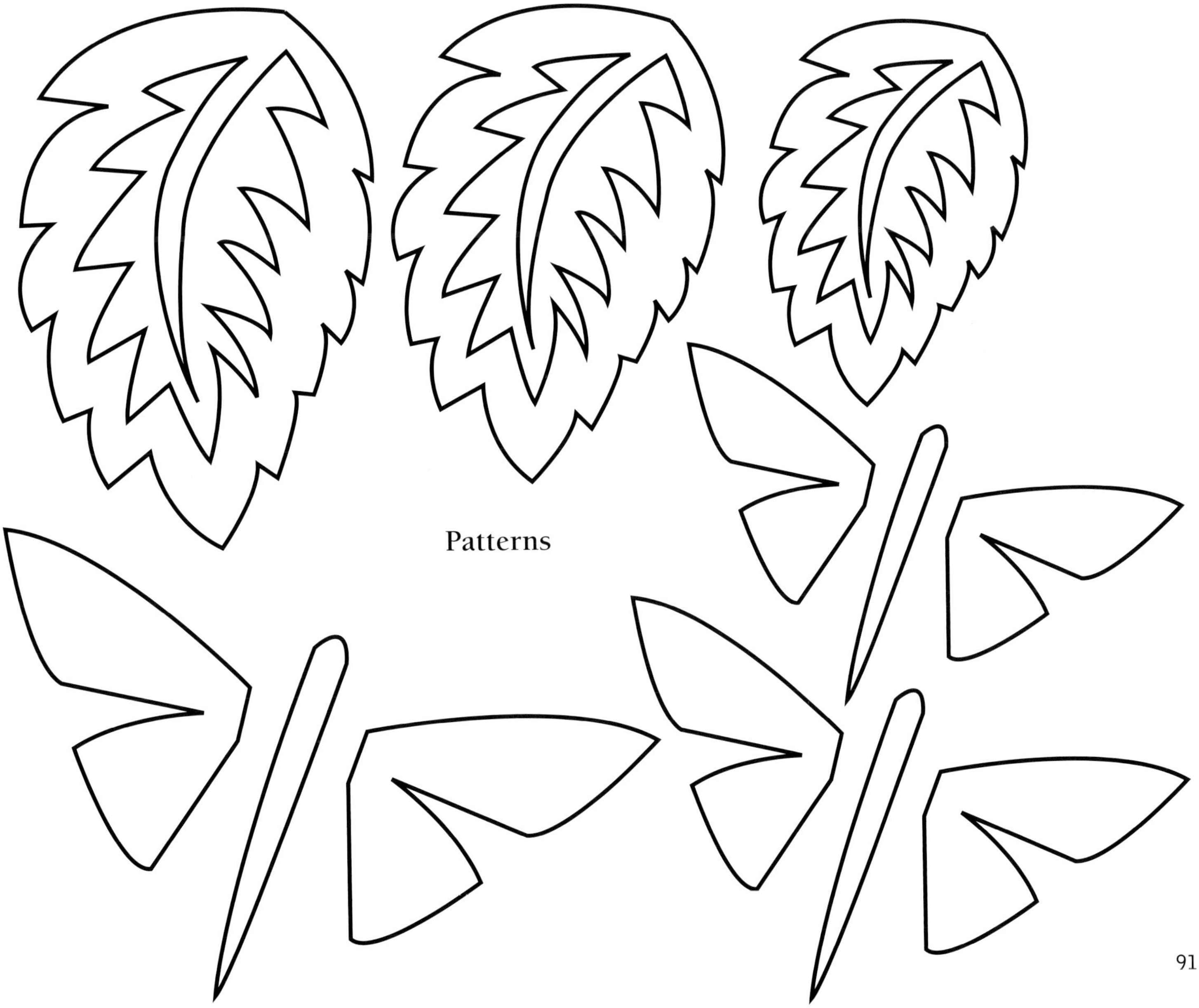

Patterns

Chapter 6

Embellishing with Sewing

This chapter includes a wealth of ideas for creating, altering, and enhancing simple garments and accessories. You'll see how to make a simple vest, turn sweaters and sweatshirts into jackets, and create fabric fringe – all with a minimum amount of sewing required.

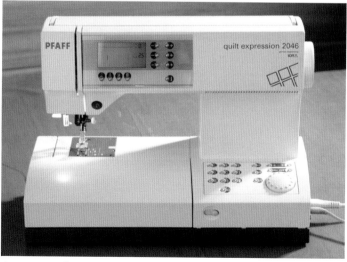

A sewing machine with straight and satin stitches is needed for these sewing projects.

Gardening Vest

See page 94 for instructions

Gardening Vest

SUPPLIES

Fabric and trim:

1 yard of cotton print fabric

1/4 yard coordinating fabric for pocket (*optional*)

5½ yards fold over trim (ours is knit ribbing trim) *Adjust amount needed if you are making your vest smaller than the one shown here.*

Thread to match

Tools & other Supplies:

Scissors

Sewing machine

Ruler

Chalk

INSTRUCTIONS

Cut the Fabric:

1. Cut 6" off from one end of your yard of fabric. This piece will be used to cut a pocket and side ties. Set this piece aside for now. (See Fig. 1) Note: You can also use a piece of coordinating fabric for pocket if you desire.

2. Cut the remaining piece in half. These pieces will be the front and back of the vest. (See Fig. 1)

3. Place the two vest pieces together, wrong sides together. Determine width you would like for each panel. For most women's sizes an 18" front and back would be a good size (petites & children need to be smaller). If your fabric panels are wider, measure, mark and cut the panels to 18" wide or to size you desire.

Pictured on page 93.

One yard of fabric, some bright trim, and an hour at your sewing machine is all you need to create this pretty and practical tabard-style vest. The cute cotton fabric with printed insects makes it the perfect fabric for a gardening vest. The vest is so quick and easy to make that you will want to make one for each of your gardening friends. But don't stop there – use kitchen motif fabric to make an apron, or colorful printed fabric to make an art and craft coverup. You can tailor this vest easily to any task or size with our helpful hints.

To make a different size front and back panel: Measure across the shoulders (not hips) to determine the width needed. You will also want to shorten the panels for smaller sizes. Measure from top of shoulder to just below stomach area to determine length. Measure, mark and cut panels.

4. Cut neck opening as shown in Fig. 2. *If you are making a different sized vest: the width of the opening should be measured from the left and right of clavicle bone (collar bone); the length is from shoulder to just below the clavicle.*

5. Cut the pieces for the pocket and the four side ties as shown in Fig. 3.

Sew the Garment:

1. Place the two vest panels, right sides together. Sew across the two shoulder seams to attach the two pieces together. Turn right side out.

2. Sew on fold-over trim along side edges and neck openings of front and back panels of the vest. Miter trim at corners.

3. Hem bottom of vest on both panels.

4. For the pocket, we doubled the fabric so it would be sturdier. Place the two pocket pieces together, right sides together. Sew pieces together, sewing along all four edges, but leaving a section for turning. Turn pocket right side out, and sew opening closed. *Adjust size for smaller vests.*

5. Sew fold-over trim to top of pocket piece, allowing about 1/2" extra trim on each side for turning under.

6. Pin pocket to vest, folding extra side trim to back. Position the pocket about 20" down from top. *Adjust position for smaller vest.* Sew in place along bottom and both sides. Use a top stitch or a fancy stitch such as a loose zig-zag. If desired, divide pocket into sections by making vertical stitches for divisions.

7. For ties, fold each tie piece in half vertically, right sides together. Sew along edges. Turn each tie right side out. Push ends to inside of ties and top stitch.

8. Sew one tie to each side of vest, front and back. Fig. 4 shows the finished vest. ◯

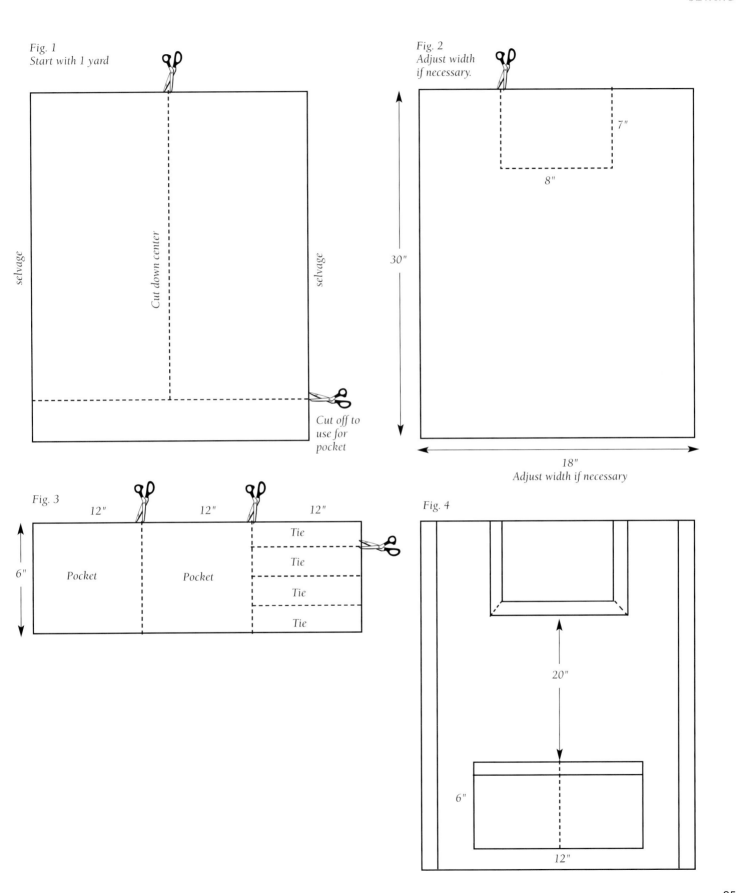

Fig. 1
Start with 1 yard

selvage

Cut down center

selvage

Cut off to use for pocket

Fig. 2
Adjust width if necessary.

7"

8"

30"

18"
Adjust width if necessary

Fig. 3

12"

12"

12"

6"

Pocket

Pocket

Tie

Tie

Tie

Tie

Fig. 4

20"

6"

12"

Panel Vest

SUPPLIES

Base:

1¹/₃ yds. corduroy

1¹/₃ yds. lining fabric

Embellishments:

2 yds. braided cording, 1/4" wide

Covered button with shank, 1/2"

Tools & Other Supplies:

Iron

Sewing machine

Cutting tools

Matching thread

Sewing needle

Make this simple vest and wear it to embellish any simple tee, top, or dress. It is easily made from two straight panels of fabric, connected at the sides with smaller rectangular panels. A fancy cord closure that you can make yourself adds the finishing touch. Cutting diagrams include measurements for petite, small, medium, large, and extra-large sizes.

by Patty Cox

INSTRUCTIONS FOR VEST

1. Using the cutting diagram (Fig. 1) as a guide, cut out the front/back, side, and back panels from both corduroy and lining fabric.
2. With right sides together and cut edges even, sew the corduroy back panel to both front/back panels.
3. With right sides together, sew a side panel to the back end of each front/back panel. Sew the side panels 3¹/₂" from the end of the front/back panel.
4. Repeat steps 2 and 3 with the lining fabric.
5. With right sides together, pin the assembled corduroy vest and lining pieces together. See Fig. 2.
6. Sew a ¹/₄" seam around the outside edges, leaving the side seams of side panels open for turning. Clip corners. Turn vest right side out through a side seam. Iron seams.

Continued on page 98

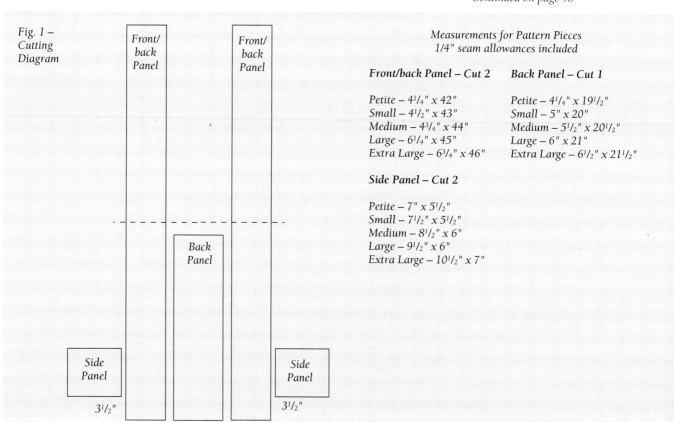

Fig. 1 – Cutting Diagram

Front/back Panel

Front/back Panel

Back Panel

Side Panel

Side Panel

3¹/₂"

3¹/₂"

Measurements for Pattern Pieces
1/4" seam allowances included

Front/back Panel – Cut 2

Petite – 4¹/₄" x 42"
Small – 4¹/₂" x 43"
Medium – 4³/₄" x 44"
Large – 6¹/₄" x 45"
Extra Large – 6³/₄" x 46"

Back Panel – Cut 1

Petite – 4¹/₄" x 19¹/₂"
Small – 5" x 20"
Medium – 5¹/₂" x 20¹/₂"
Large – 6" x 21"
Extra Large – 6¹/₂" x 21¹/₂"

Side Panel – Cut 2

Petite – 7" x 5¹/₂"
Small – 7¹/₂" x 5¹/₂"
Medium – 8¹/₂" x 6"
Large – 9¹/₂" x 6"
Extra Large – 10¹/₂" x 7"

Panel Vest

Continued from page 96

7. With right sides together, pin the ends of the corduroy side panels to the front section of the front/back panels where they were left open. Sew together with ¼" seams.

8. Turn in seam allowances of remaining lining edges. Slipstitch the lining sides together. Press seams.

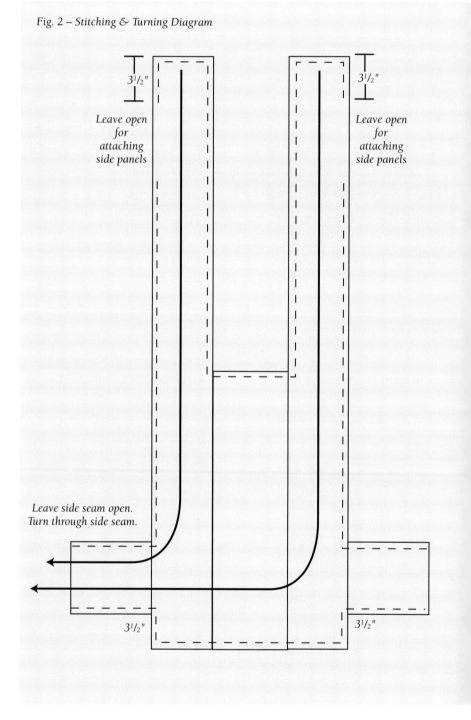

Fig. 2 – Stitching & Turning Diagram

3½"

Leave open for attaching side panels

3½"

Leave open for attaching side panels

Leave side seam open. Turn through side seam.

3½"

3½"

INSTRUCTIONS FOR CLOSURE

1. Using Fig. 3 as a guide, form the cord closure.
2. Join the loops with needle and thread. Wrap the cord ends with thread. Knot the thread before cutting the end of the cord.
3. Cover the button with fabric.
4. Sew button on one side of the closure as shown. (Fig. 4)
5. Pull one closure loop through second loop and over button as shown.
6. Position the closure on the front of the vest. Hand sew in place. ○

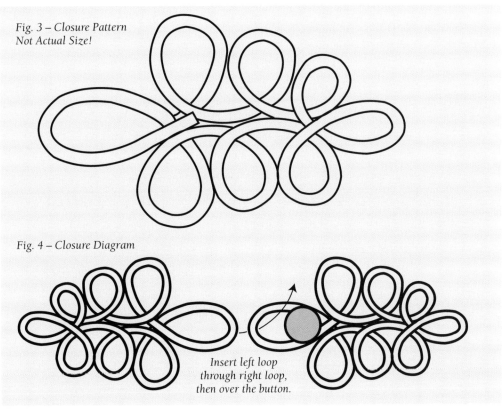

Fig. 3 – Closure Pattern Not Actual Size!

Fig. 4 – Closure Diagram

Insert left loop through right loop, then over the button.

Ruffled Tie Jacket

SUPPLIES

Base:

Long-sleeved V-neck t-shirt

Embellishments:

1 yd. sheer fabric

Tools & Other Supplies:

Thread to match shirt

Thread to match sheer fabric

Scissors

Measuring tape

Chalk pencil

Iron

Sewing machine

Safety pin

Optional: Yardstick

A long-sleeved t-shirt can be transformed into a wonderful lightweight jacket to layer over a camisole or tank top with the addition of a fabric ruffle. The sheer fabric for the ruffle makes it even more feminine and elegant. You could also use a sweatshirt as a base if you'd like a heavier jacket. See "Trimmed in Leopard" for instructions and diagrams that show how to cut a sweatshirt to make a jacket.

by Miche Baskett

INSTRUCTIONS

Alter the Shirt:

1. Use the measuring tape to determine the center point along the bottom of the front of the shirt. Mark the center point with chalk. With the chalk pencil, draw a line on the shirt from the point of the V-neck to the mark at the bottom. *Option:* Use a yardstick to make a straight line.
2. Cut along the line up the middle of the front of the shirt. Be careful to cut *only* the front – not the back – of the shirt.
3. If your shirt has ribbing around the neckline, cut it off.
4. Turn the shirt inside out. Fold the cut edges under 1/4", then fold under 1/4" again. Pin and press.

Embellish the Jacket:

1. Cut two strips of sheer fabric, each 4" x 36".
2. Fold each fabric strip in half, right sides together, aligning the long edges. Press.
3. Using matching thread, sew a seam along the long edge and one end of each folded strip. Trim the seams.
4. Place a safety pin on the seamed end of one strip and use it to turn the strip right-side out. Repeat with second strip. Press flat.
5. Turn in the open end of each strip 1/4". Press or pin in place. Stitch to close the folded edges.
6. Determine which end of each strip looks neater and nicer. With the shirt inside-out, position the fabric strips with the sewn edges along the shirt neckline Leave 11" to 12" of each strip (for the ties) dangling from the point of the V-neck. Pleat the fabric to make a ruffle fabric around the neckline as you pin it in place. The other ends should meet in the back of the neckline. Overlap the pieces with the one folded inward 1/2" to look like a pleat.

FINISH

With thread to match the shirt, sew a straight-stitched hem along all the folded edges of the jacket, attaching the ruffled fabric strip. Remove the pins as you go. Turn the shirt right side out. C

Elegant Ruched Collar

SUPPLIES

Base:

Long-sleeved crew-neck knit shirt

Embellishments:

Scarf in matching color, 5½" x 54"

Tools & Other Supplies:

Thread in matching color

Sewing machine

Scissors

Pins

A silky oblong scarf makes an elegant collar for a knitted shirt. The striking color of the shirt with its matched flouncy collar turns a casual tee into something you can wear to a fancy dinner. If you can't find a scarf to match your shirt, you could make one from 1½ yards of matching fabric or choose a scarf in a contrasting or complementary color.

by Miche Baskett

INSTRUCTIONS

1. Try on the shirt and mark how wide and how low you want the neckline to be, using the photo as a guide. Cut the neckline of the shirt to make it wider (towards the shoulders) and lower in the front according to your marks. Cut a little at a time and try it on repeatedly to make sure it is the look you desire.

2. Turn the shirt inside out. Position the scarf around neckline, right sides together, so that the ends overlap off-center on the front of the shirt. Pin the ends in place. *If you are using fabric, cut the fabric to 5½" x 54" and hem all sides with a rolled hem.*

3. To make the ruched collar, pinch pleat the scarf about every 2" to make 1" pleats to fit the scarf to the neckline. Pin the scarf in place, being careful not to stretch the neckline out of shape as you work.

4. Machine stitch around the neckline of the shirt, sewing the scarf in place and removing pins as you come to them. Use a zig-zag stitch to finish the seam.

5. Turn shirt and the collar right sides out. ⭕

Easy Ruffled Caftan

Summer time and the living is easy when you wear this light and breezy caftan. It is so easy to make and so beautiful to wear. Be the envy of your next pool party or just wear it when you want to feel beautifully relaxed. Choose a luscious cotton fabric and contrasting trim for a striking look. It takes a minimum of sewing so you can make it in a few hours. The only sewing required is making straight sides seam, hemming, and adding of the trim.

SUPPLIES

Fabric & Trim:

4 yards of cotton fabric, 36" to 42" wide

Thread to match

8' of 1½" wide grosgrain ribbon

5½' of 7/8" wide grosgrain ribbon

Tools:

Scissors

Chalk

Ruler

Sewing machine

Straight pins

INSTRUCTIONS

Cut the Fabric:

1. Determine the length you want the caftan to be. Double that measurement and cut the fabric piece to that length + 1" extra for hem. *If you are petite or small size, you will need to cut the width of your fabric to a smaller size. Don't cut the panel any narrower than 30" or the sleeve area may be too short.*

2. Fold the fabric in half with right sides together so that the selvage edges are on each side.

3. To cut the top folded edge for the neck opening, first find the center point of the front side of caftan. Beginning at the top folded edge, make a vertical cut 9" long. Then make a horizontal cut along the top folded edge, measuring 4½" each side of center. (See Fig. 1) At front neckline, cut away some fabric to make a curved neckline as shown in Fig. 2. Cut away some of the fabric at the back neckline in a curve as shown in Fig. 3.

Sew the Garment:

1. Turn garment wrong side out. Begin 12" down from top folded edge to sew the side seams on each side. (See Fig. 1.) The unsewn areas on each side are the arm openings.

2. Hem edges of arm openings. (Since the sides were the selvage edges of our fabric, we turned the hem under only one turn.)

3. Hem the bottom of garment with a double turned 1/2" hem. Top stitch hem with machine.

4. Turn garment to right side.

Embellish the Garment:

1. Cut the 1½" ribbon in half so that you have two pieces, each 4 ft. long.

2. Pin the ribbon to the sleeve edges, with the center of the ribbon at the hem of the sleeve. Pleat the ribbon as you pin it in place. Sew ribbon trim to sleeve edges along the center of the ribbon.

3. Use the same technique to fit the trim along the neckline. Start the ribbon at the center back of the garment. Sew trim in place. ○

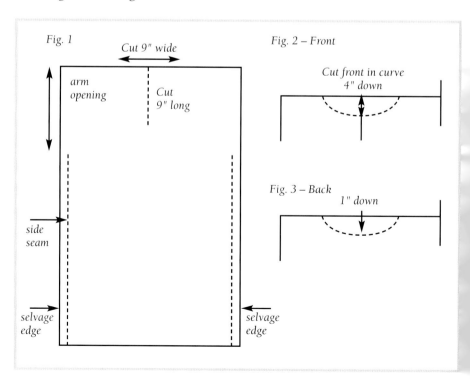

Fig. 1

Cut 9" wide

arm opening

Cut 9" long

side seam

selvage edge

selvage edge

Fig. 2 – Front

Cut front in curve
4" down

Fig. 3 – Back

1" down

Neckline Detail

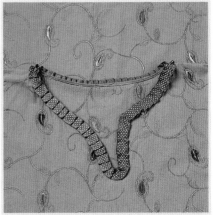

Sleeve Detail

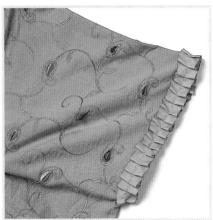

Gray Garden

SUPPLIES

Fabric & Trims:

2 yards silk fabric, 36" wide

Thread to match

Satin fabric, various shades of gray, scraps or 1/4 yd. of each color

6mm pearls (one for each yo-yo flower)

Tools & Other Supplies:

Sewing machine

Ruler

Scissors

Chalk

Straight pins

INSTRUCTIONS

Cut the Fabric:

1. Determine the length you want the caftan to be. Double that measurement and cut the fabric piece to that length + 1" extra for hem. For most sizes a 23" length would be good. Cut the width of the fabric to 22". *This width would be fine for size medium/ large. If you are petite or small size, you will need to cut the width of your fabric to a smaller size.*

2. Fold the fabric in half with right sides together so that the selvage edges are on each side.

3. To cut the top folded edge for the neck opening, first find the center point of the front side of caftan. Beginning at the top folded edge, make a mark 2½" down. Then measure 5¼" to each side of this point. Cut out a crescent shape along fold, cutting through front and back panels for neck opening as shown in Fig. 1.

Be seen in this elegant top that is so easy to make. Silky gray fabric is used to make this striking short caftan. Various shades of gray satin make the roses that trim the garment. Choose a lightweight filmy fabric for the caftan so that it hangs softly.

4. For the kimono-like sleeve, cut two pieces of fabric, each measuring 24" x 10".

Sew the Garment:

1. Turn garment to the wrong side. Begin 12" down from top folded edge to sew the side seams on each side. The unsewn areas on each side are the arm openings.

2. Hem three sides of each sleeve piece with a rolled hem. See Fig. 2.

3. Turn garment to right side. Pin the cut edge of one of the sleeve pieces to one of the arm opening, with right sides together. Sew sleeve to arm opening. The sleeve will be open at the bottom to create a kimono-like look.

4. Hem the bottom of garment with a double turned 1/2" hem. Top stitch hem with machine.

Make Fabric Roses:

1. For each large rose, cut from satin, a 3" x 50" (or width of fabric) strip. Fold strip in half lengthwise.

2. Sew 1/4" seam along each end. (Fig. 3) Turn right side out.

3. Sew long gathering stitches along the long raw edges of the strip. (Fig. 4) Pull the threads to gather strip to a length of about 30".

4. Tightly coil one end of the strip to form the rose center. (Fig. 5) Sew the coiled raw edges together with needle and thread.

5. Loosely coil the remaining gathered strip around the center, sewing the raw edges together as you turn the rose.

6. For smaller roses, cut strips 3" x 20". Make roses following steps 1-5.

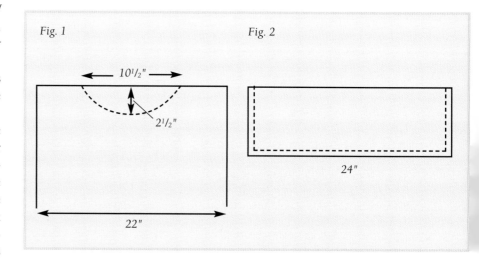

Fig. 1

10½"

2½"

22"

Fig. 2

24"

Make Flat Yo-Yo Flowers:

1. Cut 2" circles from satin fabric. Cut one circle for each flower you wish to make.
2. Use a needle and thread to sew 1/8" long running stitches 1/8" from the edge of one circle. Pull the gathers tight. Knot the thread on the back of the gathered yo-yo. Flatten yo-yo.
3. Insert the needle into the yo-yo center. Add a 6mm pearl bead. Knot thread on yo-yo back.
4. Repeat steps 2 and 3 to complete all the yo-yo flowers.

Embellish the Garment:

Sew the roses and yo-yo flowers to the neckline of the garment. ⭕

Fig. 3

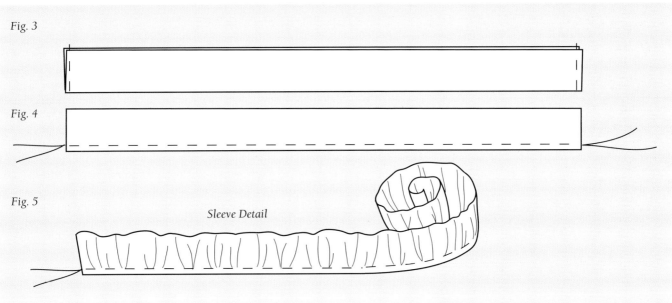

Fig. 4

Fig. 5

Sleeve Detail

Trimmed in Leopard

SUPPLIES

Base:

Long-sleeved fleece top *or* sweatshirt

Embellishments:

2½ yds.* (approx.) leopard print ribbon, 1" wide

Leopard print sash *or* narrow scarf, at least 48" long *or* fabric to make a tie.

4 brown and white buttons

Tools & Other Supplies:

Thread to match top

Thread to match ribbon

Chalk pencil

Measuring tape

Sewing needle *or* sewing machine

Scissors

Straight pins

Iron

Optional: Yardstick

* To determine the amount of ribbon you need, measure around the neckline, center fronts, hem, and sleeves of the top you want to use.

INSTRUCTIONS

Alter the Top:

1. Use a measuring tape and chalk to measure, then mark the halfway point along the front bottom of the top. Make another mark at the halfway point along the front neckline.

2. With the chalk pencil, draw a line from the mark on the neckline to the mark at the bottom. (Fig. 1) *TIP:* Use a yardstick to make a straight line.

This warm, comfy and stylish jacket started as a sweatshirt-style fleece top. Leopard print ribbon and a leopard print sash come together to add style to the garment.

by Miche Baskett

3. Cut open the front of the shirt along the marked line. Be careful to cut only the front, **not the back**, of the shirt.

4. Cut off all ribbing and round the neckline to create a V-shape. (Fig. 2)

Continued on page 110

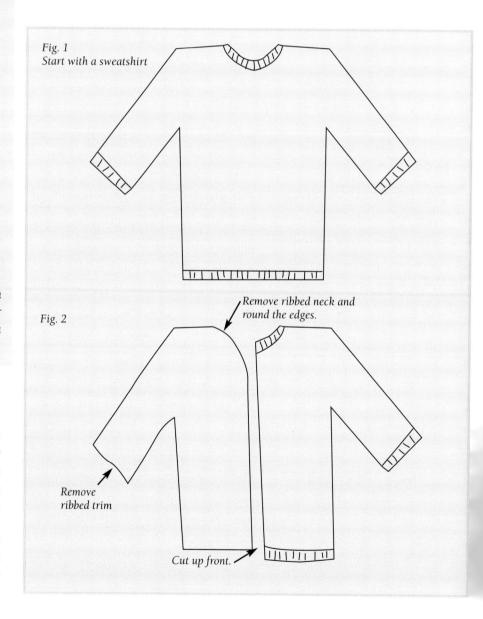

Fig. 1
Start with a sweatshirt

Fig. 2

Remove ribbed neck and round the edges.

Remove ribbed trim

Cut up front.

Trimmed in Leopard

Continued from page 108

5. Fold under the cut edges of the neckline, front edges, and bottom 1/4". Press. Turn under 1/4" again. Pin and press. Sew with matching thread, removing the pins as you go.

6. If you cut ribbing off the sleeves, use the same process to hem the sleeves.

Embellish the Jacket:

1. Position ribbon around the sleeves, along the bottom edge of the jacket, up both sides of the front, and around the neckline, using the photo as a guide. Miter the ribbon at the corners and pin in place. (Fig. 3)

2. Stitch along both edges of the ribbon to attach it to the jacket, using thread that matches the ribbon.

3. If your sash or scarf is 48" long, cut it in half. If it's longer, measure 24" from each end of the sash and mark. Cut off the two 24" ends. Discard the middle of the sash or save for another sewing project. *Alternately, sew fabric to make two tie pieces that are 24" long by 3¹/₂" wide.*

4. Pleat or gather the cut end of each sash piece.

5. Pin the pleated or gathered ends of the sash pieces inside the jacket fronts about 8" from the bottom of the jacket. Try on the jacket to check the placement and to be sure the sash pieces line up properly. Adjust as needed.

6. Using the thread that matches the ribbon, sew the sash pieces in place, stitching along the line where you sewed the ribbon.

7. Sew the buttons on in a pleasing arrangement. (I placed two buttons near the sash on each side.) ○

Fig. 3

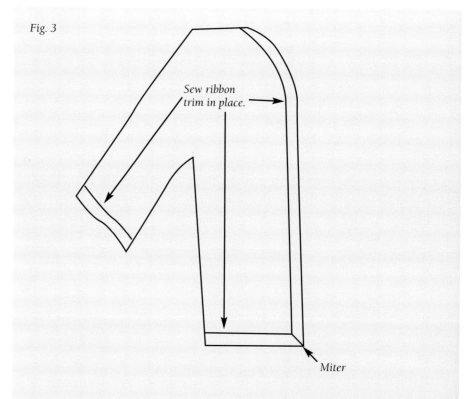

Sew ribbon trim in place.

Miter

Fig. 4

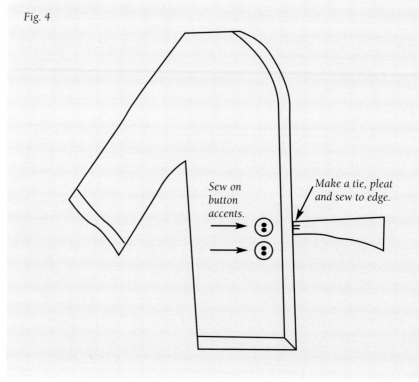

Sew on button accents.

Make a tie, pleat and sew to edge.

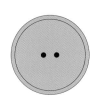

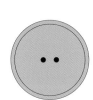

Chapter 7

Embellishing with Cutwork

Sometimes, rather than adding something to a garment, embellishing involves taking something away. This chapter shows inventive embellishing techniques with cutwork – a process of cutting away fabric with scissors or a craft knife to create designs and motifs. A sewing machine is needed for stabilizing the cutouts. Some projects are stitched before cutting, some afterward.

Lacy Sophisticated Suit

SUPPLIES

Base:

Linen suit

Tools & Other Supplies:

Matching thread

Small, sharp-pointed scissors

Embroidery hoop

Tear-away stabilizer *or* press-and-seal plastic wrap

Tracing paper and pencil

Transfer paper and stylus

Sewing machine capable of making a fine satin stitch (use a satin edge, over-edge, or embroidery presser foot)

INSTRUCTIONS

1. Trace the patterns and transfer the design to the garment (See page 114).
2. Place stabilizer or press-and-seal wrap on the wrong side of the jacket under the transferred design.
3. Working one area at a time, place the design area in an embroidery hoop. Machine straight stitch on the design lines.
4. Set sewing machine for a narrow satin stitch. Satin stitch over the straight-stitched design lines.
5. Remove embroidery hoop and press-and-seal wrap or stabilizer.
6. Using small, sharp-pointed scissors, cut away the fabric within stitched design, being careful not to cut into the satin stitching. ○

A plain linen suit is given designer status with lacy cutwork flowers sprinkled across the top.

by Patty Cox

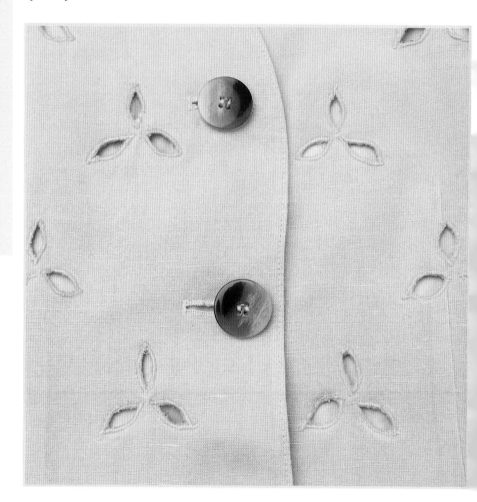

Lacy Sophisticated Suit

Continued from page 112

Pattern

Roses on Denim
See page 116 for instructions.

Pattern

Roses on Denim Skirt

SUPPLIES

Base:

Denim skirt

Embellishments:

4 squares colored fabric, each 6" –
    Red, rust, orange, green

Tools & Other Supplies:

Fabric glue

Scissors

Sharp craft knife

Sewing machine

Tracing paper and pencil

Transfer paper and stylus

Wax paper

Thread to match denim

A simple denim skirt is adorned with cutwork roses in three colors and simple green leaves. When you wash the skirt, the cutout areas will fray slightly, enhancing the casual look.

by Patty Cox

INSTRUCTIONS

1. Trace the pattern and transfer to the skirt (See page 115).
2. Cut away the cutwork designs with scissors or a sharp craft knife.
3. Trim the colored fabric pieces to fit the cutout areas + 1/4" all around.
4. Cover your work surface with a piece of wax paper. Lay the cut area flat on the wax paper, wrong side up. Spread a thin layer of fabric glue 1/4" wide around all cut out areas.
5. Place the colored fabric pieces, wrong sides up, over the cutout areas. Trim the colored fabrics, if needed, to 1/4" from the cutout areas. Allow glue to dry.
6. Machine straight stitch around all edges of the cutouts, 1/8" from the edge. ○

Peek a Boo Dress

SUPPLIES

Base:

Cotton dress, plain color

Tools & Other Supplies:

Chalk pencil

Ruler

Tear-away stabilizer

Sewing machine capable of making a
fine satin stitch (use a satin edge,
over-edge, or embroidery presser
foot)

Thread to match dress (or contrasting
thread for more color)

Small sharp-pointed scissors

Poster board

Craft knife

INSTRUCTIONS

1. Mark off your dress vertically and
horizontally with rows 2¼" apart.
See Fig. 1. Start by finding the center
vertically and measure and mark
lines to both sides of center. For horizontal rows, begin at shoulder and
work down.

2. Using a ruler and craft knife, make a
template from poster board with a
3/4" square cut out.

3. Where the marked lines intersect on
the dress, position the template over
alternating intersections so it's centered where the lines cross, and trace
around the 3/4" square with your
chalk pencil. Be sure to stagger the positions of the squares. Refer to Fig. 1.

4. Reinforce the back of the design area
with tear-away stabilizer.

5. With your sewing machine, make a
straight stitch directly over the
chalked design lines.

Scissors turn this plain black sundress into a show-stopper. Layering the
dress over colorful leggings and a tee adds to the fun, or be flirty and
layer it over colorful lingerie. This is time consuming but easy, and well
worth the effort.

6. Set your sewing machine for a narrow satin stitch. Sew a satin stitch
over the drawn chalk lines of each
marked square. Continue until you
have sewn the outline of each square.

7. Using the small sharp-pointed scissors, cut away the fabric within the
stitched lines of the squares. Be **very
careful** when doing this so you do
not cut into the stitching.

Alternative Method: Some find it easier
to cut out the design and then satin
stitch around the cut out area. If you are
doing this, you must have the special
presser foot so that the satin stitches do
not bunch up and distort the fabric. Follow previous instructions through #6.
Then cut out the design, cutting away
the fabric and the stabilizer inside the
design, Cut close to the straight
stitches. Then satin stitch around the
edge of the design. We recommend that
you practice both methods on a scrap
piece of paper before attempting the
technique on your garment. ❍

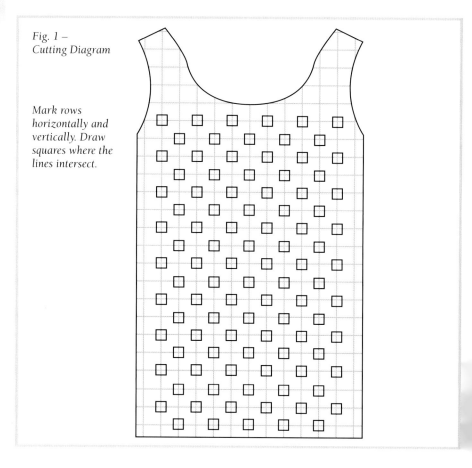

*Fig. 1 –
Cutting Diagram*

*Mark rows
horizontally and
vertically. Draw
squares where the
lines intersect.*

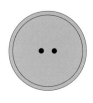

Chapter 8

Embellishing with Trims & Accents

This chapter shows a variety of ideas for embellishing with buttons and braid and fringe you can buy by the yard at fabric and crafts stores. You'll also see how to use natural leather, fabric flowers, and pom poms you make yourself from yarn to enhance all kinds of wearables.

Trimmed with Leather

SUPPLIES

Base:

Denim shirt

Embellishments:

Saddle tan doeskin, 19" x 36"

7 yds. leather lacing, 5/32"

Tools & Other Supplies:

Fabric glue (or contact leather cement)

Leather hole punch

Seam ripper

Scissors

Sewing needle and thread

INSTRUCTIONS

Cut & Glue:

1. Remove the buttons and collar from the denim shirt. If necessary, re-shape the neckline so it looks like the one in the project photo.
2. Measure the front length of the shirt and the distance around each cuff. Compare these measurements to those on the Cutting Diagram (Fig. 1).
3. Cut the doeskin according to the Cutting Diagram and your shirt measurements.
4. Apply a 2" wide stripe of fabric glue around the shirt neckline. Place the shoulders and back piece of the skin around the neckline over the glue.
5. Apply a 2" wide stripe of fabric glue along both center front edges of the shirt. Place the doeskin cutouts over the glue.
6. Apply a 2" wide stripe of fabric glue around the end of each cuff. Wrap the skin cuffs over the glue. Allow glue to dry.

The irregular outer edges of a doeskin are used as a design element in the creation of this simple shirt jacket – that starts with a denim shirt. Leather lacing adds detail accenting. Only simple hand sewing is required. The measurements on the Cutting Diagram are for a medium size shirt. Modify them as needed to accommodate your shirt.

by Patty Cox

Stitch:

1. Measure and mark 1/2" from the front and neckline edges and the bottom edges of the cuffs in 1/2" increments.
2. Punch holes through the skin and shirt, using a leather punch.
3. Cut approximately 5 yards of leather lacing. Cut one end at an angle for easier threading.
4. Whipstitch the front and neck edges through the punched holes with leather lacing. Glue lacing ends inside the shirt. Secure each end with needle and thread.
5. Cut 1 yard leather lacing. Whipstitch each cuff edge with leather lacing through the punched holes. Glue lace ends on insides of cuffs. Secure each end with needle and thread. ○

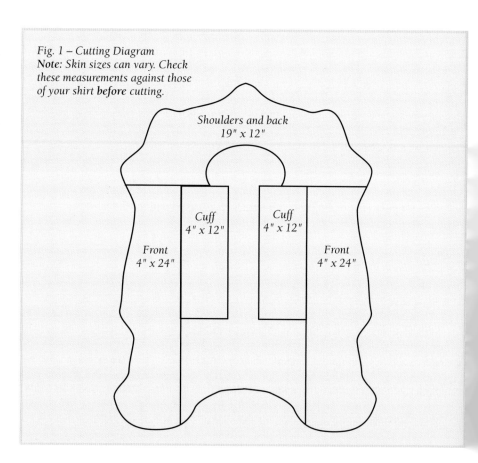

Fig. 1 – Cutting Diagram
*Note: Skin sizes can vary. Check these measurements against those of your shirt **before** cutting.*

Shoulders and back
19" x 12"

Cuff
4" x 12"

Cuff
4" x 12"

Front
4" x 24"

Front
4" x 24"

Fancy Fringed Tote

SUPPLIES

Base:

Tote bag

Embellishments:

1/4 yd. *each* of 3 colors of woven fabric

Tools & Other Supplies:

Pins

Scissors

Thread to match fringe fabrics

Sewing needle *or* sewing machine

Iron

Fray preventative liquid

Making your own fabric fringe is easy, and you can have just the colors you want.

by Phyllis Dobbs

INSTRUCTIONS

Make the Fringe:

1. Cut three fabric strips – one from each color fabric – as wide as twice the width of your tote bag plus 1" and 2¼" long.
2. Turn under one long edge of each fabric strip 1/4" and press.
3. Pull the threads away on the long edge of one fabric strip to make the fringe. See "Fringing Fabric" below. Keep pulling threads until the fringe is 1⅓" deep.
4. Repeat the process with the remaining two fabric strips. When fringing is complete, press each strip, pressing fringe flat and straight. TIP: Use a straight pin as a comb to straighten the fringe.
5. Apply fray preventive along the top of the fringed area to keep any more threads from pulling out.

Sew in Place:

1. Align the top of the fringed strip around the tote bag 1" below the top edge. Sew to bag. When you are near the end of the strip, turn the strip fabric under 1/2" and overlap the other end of the fringe.
2. Align the second strip under the first strip and sew.
3. Repeat for the third strip. ○

Fringing Fabric

This technique works only with straight woven fabrics. A loosely woven fabric is much easier to fringe than a very tightly woven one.

1. Cut a strip of fabric the length and width needed. Be sure to cut it straight along the weave.
2. Turn under one long edge 1/4" and press.
3. Loosen and gently pull the long thread at the bottom of the strip to start fringing. (Photo 1) *TIP:* Use a straight pin to separate and loosen each thread from the fabric as you pull. If the thread breaks, use tweezers to help find and pull the thread.

Photo 1 – Removing threads.

Photo 2 – Applying fray preventive liquid.

4. Keep removing threads until the fringe is as deep as you want it to be *or* until you are 1/4" from the folded top edge.

5. Squeeze fray preventive liquid along the top of the fringe to keep remaining threads from pulling out. (Photo 2)

Feathered Fringed Purse

Three purchased fringes – feather fringe, bead fringe, and shiny metallic spangle fringe – cover a canvas bag.

by Miche Baskett

SUPPLIES

Base:
Canvas purse with woven straps, 9" x 7"

Embellishments:

2 yds. feather fringe – 1 yd. each of two complementary colors

3 yds. bead fringe in colors to complement feathers – 1 yd. of three different styles

1 yd. shiny metallic shapes fringe in colors to complement the feathers and beads

Tools & Other Supplies:

Fray preventive

Fabric glue

Measuring tape

Scissors

Tape

INSTRUCTIONS

Cut the Fringe:
Apply fray preventive to both ends of each piece immediately after cutting.

1. Cut a piece of the metallic shapes fringe as long as the handle of the purse. Set aside.
2. Cut the feather fringe, bead fringe and remaining metallic shapes fringe into pieces 9½" long.

Apply:

1. Arrange the fringe pieces on the purse, layering the feathers and the beads. See the photo for ideas. Turn under the cut ends and tape in place.
2. Tape the piece of metallic shapes fringe you cut for the handle to the handle.
3. Glue the fringe to the purse and handle with fabric glue. Let dry. ◯

Button-Trimmed Purse

An array of buttons – all the same type and color but in a variety of sizes – makes a geometric statement on a simple cloth bag. Use embroidery floss that matches the buttons or, for fun, try a contrasting color.

by Miche Baskett

SUPPLIES

Base:

Fabric purse *or* messenger bag, 15"

Embellishments:

28 red pearlized shell buttons, 1"

28 red pearlized shell buttons, 3/4"

12 red pearlized shell buttons, 5/8"

2 red pearlized shell buttons, 7/16"

Tools & Other Supplies:

Embroidery floss

Chalk pencil

Ruler

Sewing needle

Scissors

INSTRUCTIONS

1. Use a ruler and chalk pencil to draw a vertical line down the center of the purse. Draw six vertical lines on each side of the center line, spacing them 1" apart.

2. With embroidery floss, sew buttons along the lines, simply looping embroidery floss through the holes in each button one time and then moving on to the next button. Work from the center line outward and from the bottom up on each line.

   Center line – ten 1" buttons

   Line left of center – eight 1" buttons

   Next line left – one 1" button on the bottom, six 3/4" buttons

   Next line left – six 3/4" buttons

   Next line left – six 3/4" buttons

   Next line left – two 3/4" buttons, three 5/8" buttons

   Next line left – three 5/8" buttons

   Last line left – one 7/16" button

   Knot the floss to secure and trim.

3. Repeat the pattern to complete the lines on the right side of the center line. ❍

Random Buttons Sweater

Buttons are washable, colorful, and easy to change accents for all kinds of garments and accessories. Because these buttons are for embellishment only, they don't need to be sewn as securely as buttons used as fasteners.

by Miche Baskett

SUPPLIES

Base:

V-neck lightweight sweater *or* tee

Embellishments:

50 (approx.) small clear pearlized buttons

15 buttons, various sizes and colors

Tools & Other Supplies:

Embroidery floss to match sweater

Thread to match colored buttons

Chalk pencil

Ruler

Sewing needle

Scissors

Safety pins

INSTRUCTIONS

1. Use a ruler and chalk pencil to draw a zig-zag line around the neckline of the sweater.
2. Using embroidery floss, sew the clear pearlized buttons all along the zig-zag line. Simply loop the floss through the holes in each button one time, and then move on to the next button. See the photo for placement.
3. Arrange the other buttons around the zig-zag, using the photo as a guide. Hold each button in place with a safety pin.
4. Sew the remaining buttons in place using thread to match each button. Remove safety pins as you go. You only need to loop the thread through the holes in the buttons a few times. ◯

Lacy to a T

A plain ecru v-neck t-shirt takes on an elegant air when you add lace trim and flowers cut from antique doilies. (It's a good way to use all those moldering doilies you can't throw away.) It's so easy to make your clothes special with just a few little tricks with trim.

SUPPLIES

Base:

V-neck ecru t-shirt

Embellishments:

1 yard of 1½" wide flat ecru lace (or enough to cover neckline ribbing)

Motifs cut from antique doilies for pieces of lace trim

Thread to match

Tools & Other Supplies:

Scissors

Sewing needle

Fray preventative

INSTRUCTIONS

1. Measure and cut enough flat lace to cover the neckline ribbing. Apply fray preventative to both cut ends of the lace. Sew lace to the neckline ribbing using a running stitch along both sides of the lace. *TIP:* Start and end at center back of neckline, turning under ends and stitching ends in place.
2. Cut out motifs from doilies or pieces of lace trim. Apply fray preventative to the cut areas of pieces.
3. Sew motifs to the garment as desired, using a running stitch or whip stitch around edges of motifs. ○

Button-Down Dress

SUPPLIES

Base:

Jumper dress

Embellishments:

16 small brown buttons, same size and color

20 (approx.) buttons, various sizes and colors

Tools & Other Supplies:

Thread to match colored buttons

Chalk pencil

Ruler

Sewing needle

Scissors

Safety pins

INSTRUCTIONS

1. Use a ruler and chalk pencil to draw four diamonds down the center front of the dress. Use the photo as a guide for placement.

2. Sew a small brown button at each corner of each diamond shape – simply loop the thread through the holes of each button a few times, then move on to the next button.

3. Position the remaining various buttons around the collar and along the hem of the dress in a pleasing arrangement. See the photo for ideas. Hold each button in place with a safety pin.

4. Sew the buttons one at a time, using thread to match the button, removing the safety pins as you go. ○

Buttons sewn in the shape of diamonds decorate the bodice of a consignment store purchase sleeveless dress. More buttons in a variety of colors and sizes accent the hem and the neckline. Because these buttons are used as embellishments they don't need to be sewn as securely as buttons used as fasteners.

by Miche Baskett

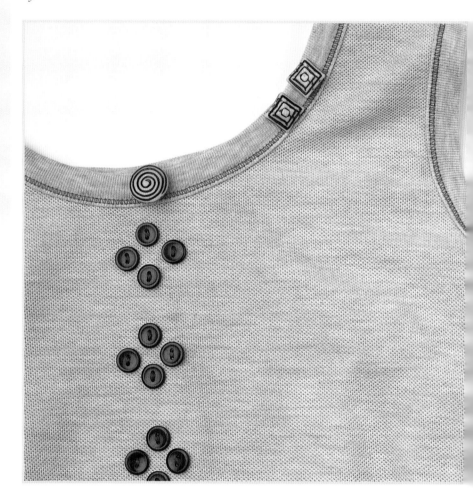

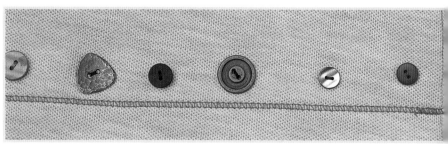

Hemline

Pom Pom Purse

SUPPLIES

Base:

1/2 yd. embroidered silk fabric
1/2 yd. lining fabric
Rattan handles
Matching thread

Embellishments:

2 skeins coordinating yarn

Tools & Other Supplies:

Pompom tool *or* cardboard piece cut 2" wide
Sewing needle and thread
Scissors
Sewing machine
Iron

INSTRUCTIONS

Cut:

1. Cut two pieces of silk fabric, each 13" x 15", for the front and back.
2. Cut two pieces of lining fabric the same size.
3. Cut a strip of silk fabric 3" x 12" for the handle loops.

Make the Bag:

1. With right sides facing, sew the silk pieces together on the bottom and sides, using a 1/2" seam allowance.
2. Repeat with the lining fabric.
3. To create a flat bottom, open out corner by placing the bottom seam on top of the side seam. Sew across the corner to create a flat bottom for the bag. Repeat on the other side and with the lining. See Fig. 1.
4. Turn the silk fabric right side out. Press the edges of the open end under 1/2". Press the edges of the open end of the lining under 1/2".
5. Place the lining inside the silk fabric, aligning the side seams, and pin together. Set aside.

Fluffy pom poms add flair to this Asian-inspired bag with rattan handles made from embroidered silk fabric. Use it as a purse or to carry your favorite book or needlework project or even your lunch! We've included instructions for making the bag itself; you could also buy a bag and embellish it with embroidery and pom poms. The finished size of the bag is 12" x 14".

by Pattie Donham

Add the Handles:

1. Fold the strip of silk fabric lengthwise, with right sides facing. Sew a 1/2" seam the entire length of the piece.
2. Turn right side out. Cut into four equal pieces.
3. Thread each piece through the handle ends and baste the raw edges together.
4. Pin the handle loops to the top of the bag between the lining and the silk fabric.
5. Topstitch the top of the bag all the way around to secure handles and sew the lining in place.

Add the Pom Poms:

1. Make 10, pom poms that measure 2" diameter, using the two colors of yarn as one as you wrap. Follow the "How to Make a Pompom" instructions.
2. Sew the pom poms around the bag 3" from the top. ◯

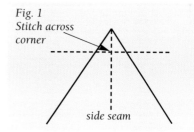

Fig. 1
Stitch across corner
side seam

How to Make a Pom Pom

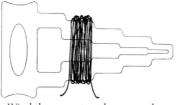

1. *Wind the yarns together around pompom tool (or piece of 2" wide cardboard) 25 times on the 2" tier of the tool.*

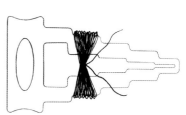

2. *Cut 8" of yarn and use it to tie the center of the pompom very tightly.*

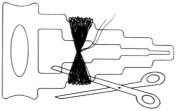

3. *Use scissors to cut both sides of the pompom to release it from the tool.*

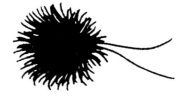

4. *Shake out the pompom and trim it evenly into a nice round shape.*

Pom Poms a Pied

SUPPLIES

Base:

Flip flops

Embellishments:

6 yds. white tulle, 6" wide

6 yds. plaid ribbon, 5/8" wide

Clear rhinestones

Tools & Other Supplies:

Pompom tool *or* cardboard cut 3" wide

20 gauge wire

Craft glue

Wire cutters

Scissors

INSTRUCTIONS

Make the Pom Poms:

See "How to Make a Pompom" on page 132.

1. Cut 3 yds. ribbon and 3 yds. tulle.
2. Wind them together around the pompom tool on the 3" tier of the tool.
3. Cut a 6" piece of wire. Wrap the center of the pompom tightly with wire, then twist the wire.
4. Cut both sides of the pompom with scissors to release it from the tool.
5. Shake out the pompom and trim it evenly into a nice round shape.
6. Repeat steps 1 through 5 to make a second pompom.

If you are using a 3" piece of cardboard to make the pom poms: wind the ribbon and tulle together around the cardboard 25 times. Pull the yarn off the cardboard, wrap the center with wire, twist the wire, and cut the loops. Shake out the pompom and trim into a round shape.

These kitten-heeled flip flops will set your toes to tapping when you add puffy pom poms made with tulle, ribbon, and rhinestones. No wallflowers here!

by Pattie Donham

Attach & Decorate the Pom Poms:

1. Attach a pompom to each flip flop with wire. Be careful to turn the ends of the wire into the pom poms.
2. Glue rhinestones to the edges of the pom poms ○

Sparkly Summer Shoes

Creating a custom look for a special outfit or color combination couldn't be easier – simply cut and glue!

by Miche Baskett

SUPPLIES

Base:

Black sandals with a wide cloth band

Embellishments:

1/2 yd. *each* of four types of ribbon or braid in coordinating colors and various widths

Tools & Other Supplies:

Fabric glue

Scissors

Measuring tape

INSTRUCTIONS

1. Test the fabric glue on a small section of each type of braid and ribbon to make sure the glue will not show through the other side. Allow to dry. Continue if results are satisfactory.
2. Measure the band of the sandal to determine how long to cut the pieces you need.
3. Cut two pieces of each type of ribbon or braid (one for each sandal) to the determined length plus 1/2".
4. Arrange the ribbon and braid pieces on the bands of the sandals. See the photo for examples.
5. Working one piece at a time, glue the ribbon and braid pieces in place. Allow the adhesive to dry before you add another piece. Repeat until all the pieces are glued to both sandals.
6. After all the glue has dried, carefully trim away any excess ribbon or braid. ❍

Crochet Trimmed Hoodie

SUPPLIES

83 yards of 100& nylon multi-colored #5 bulky fashion texture yarn

Size G Crochet Hook

Simple crochet trim gives this knitted hoodie extra pizzazz. There are so many fun yarns available, you'll want to trim all your sweaters.

by Sue Penrod

INSTRUCTIONS

GAUGE: sc, ch 1 = 7 pattern stitch = 3 inches.

Crochet in sweater ribbing, working between the ribs

1. Row 1: Sl st, sc, ch 1 skip the next sweater rib, sc, *ch 1, sc repeat from *around sweater
2. Row 2: Ch 2 and turn, sc in next ch1 sp, *ch 2, sc in next ch1 sp, repeat from *around.
3. Fasten off, tucking ends.

Crochet Stitches

Slip Stitch (sl st)

The crochet needle has a loop already on it. It is then placed into another loop. Yarn is placed over the hook and pulled through the loop and the loop on the hook.

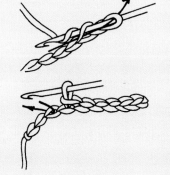

Chain Stitch (ch)

To begin the chain, make a loop around needle, then pull another loop through that loop. With a stitch (or loop) on the hook, yarn is wrapped around the needle. The hook pulls the yarn through the loop on the hook.

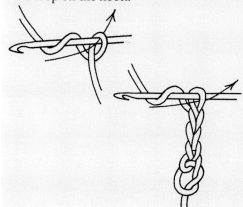

Single Crochet (sc)

There must first be three chain loops as a foundation, counting the one on the hook. The hook is inserted into the 2nd stitch from the needle (not counting the one on the hook). Yarn is placed over the hook and is pulled through the stitch loop plus the loop on the needle.

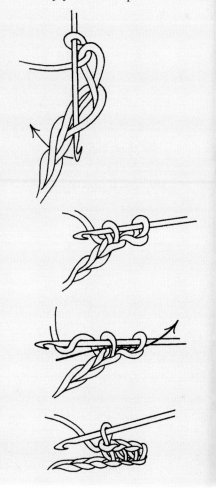

Sweet Flowers & Pearls Sweater

SUPPLIES

Base:

Blue sweater

Embellishments:

1/2 yd. light gray satin fabric

White pearl beads, 6mm

White pearl beads, 3mm

Tools & Other Supplies:

Sewing needle and thread

Tracing paper and pencil

Transfer paper and stylus

Scissors

INSTRUCTIONS

Make the Yo-Yo Roses:

1. Cut 2" circles from satin fabric, using the pattern provided. (We used about 70 flowers for our sweater.)
2. Use a needle and thread to sew 1/8" long running stitches 1/8" from the edge of one circle. Pull the gathers tight. Knot the thread on the back of the gathered yo-yo.
3. Insert the needle into the yo-yo center. Add a 6mm pearl bead. Knot thread on yo-yo back.
4. Repeat steps 2 and 3 to complete all the yo-yo roses.

Embellish the Sweater:

1. Hand sew the yo-yo roses around the neck edge of the sweater, positioning them close together.
2. Again positioning them close together, sew yo-yo roses around the bottom of each sleeve.

Satin yo-yo flowers and pearl beads dress up a cardigan sweater. For best results, choose a simple sweater with minimal ribbing at the neckline, sleeve ends, and hem. If your sweater didn't come with pearl buttons, consider replacing them.

by Patty Cox

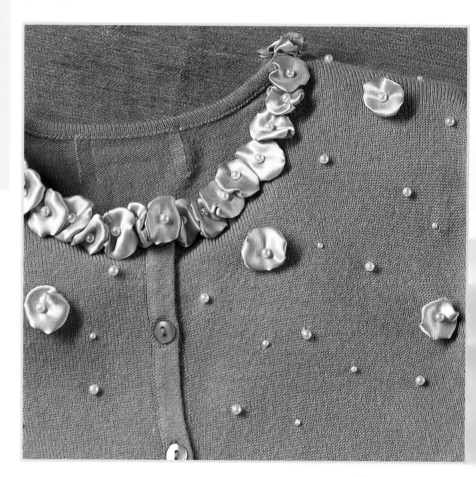

3. Arrange six (or more) roses on the upper areas of the sweater as shown in the project photo. Sew in place.
4. Arrange and sew 6mm pearls and 3mm pearls around the roses. ○

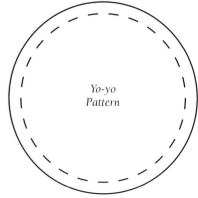

Yo-yo Pattern

Satin Rose Purse

SUPPLIES

Base:

Black fabric purse with flap

Embellishments:

1/2 yd. pewter satin fabric

Tools & Other Supplies:

Sewing needle and thread

Optional: Sewing machine, fabric glue

A softly gathered satin strip is coiled to form a rose. We've shown it on a fabric purse – you could also use it to adorn a hat or wear it on your lapel.

by Patty Cox

INSTRUCTIONS

1. Cut 3" x 50" satin strip. Fold strip in half lengthwise.
2. Sew 1/4" seam along each end. (Fig. 1) Turn right side out.
3. Sew long gathering stitches along the long raw edges of the strip. (Fig. 2) Pull the threads to gather strip to a length of about 30".
4. Tightly coil one end of the strip to form the rose center. (Fig. 3) Sew the coiled raw edges together with needle and thread.
5. Loosely coil the remaining gathered strip around the center, sewing the raw edges together as you turn the rose.
6. Sew the rose on the flap of the purse *or* glue in place with fabric glue. ○

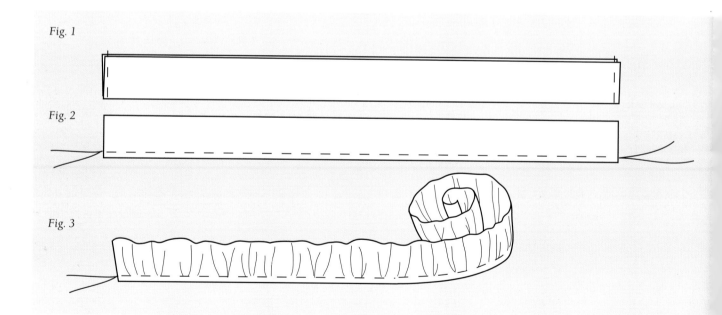

Fig. 1

Fig. 2

Fig. 3

Trimmed with a Scarf

SUPPLIES

Base:

V-neck shirt

Embellishments:

Narrow oblong scarf, length

Tools & Other Supplies:

Thread to match shirt

Sewing needle

Scissors

Straight pins

INSTRUCTIONS

Converting the Shirt:

1. Pin the collar to the band on the right side of the shirt. Sew the collar down along the bottom stitches of the band. Trim off the excess fabric. The scarf will cover the cut ends. Save the excess fabric to make a neck closure.

2. With the excess fabric, make a small fabric strip measuring about 2" long x 3/8" wide. Hem the edges or make it double so that seams are on inside of strip.

3. Sew one end of the strip to the inside of the collar band. Attach the other end to the inside of the collar band with buttons, hooks, or hook and loop closure so that it can be detached when taking the shirt on and off.

Add the Scarf:

1. Knot the scarf all along its length, leaving about 3" between the knots.

2. Place the scarf around the collar of the shirt, with the ends hanging in front. Pin in place.

3. Sew the scarf to the collar of the shirt

This shirt had a collar on the collar band. I liked the shirt, but not the collar, so I changed it before adding the knotted scarf trim. Choose a scarf with a design and colors that coordinate with shirt.

by Miche Baskett

by stitching from the inside of the collar through each knot in the scarf. (If you're careful, the stitches will be invisible from the outside.)

4. Remove all pins and trim excess threads. ○

Metric Conversion Chart

Inches to Millimeters and Centimeters

Inches	MM	CM	Inches	MM	CM
1/8	3	.3	2	51	5.1
1/4	6	.6	3	76	7.6
3/8	10	1.0	4	102	10.2
1/2	13	1.3	5	127	12.7
5/8	16	1.6	6	152	15.2
3/4	19	1.9	7	178	17.8
7/8	22	2.2	8	203	20.3
1	25	2.5	9	229	22.9
1-1/4	32	3.2	10	254	25.4
1-1/2	38	3.8	11	279	27.9
1-3/4	44	4.4	12	305	30.5

Yards to Meters

Yards	Meters	Yards	Meters
1/8	.11	3	2.74
1/4	.23	4	3.66
3/8	.34	5	4.57
1/2	.46	6	5.49
5/8	.57	7	6.40
3/4	.69	8	7.32
7/8	.80	9	8.23
1	.91	10	9.14
2	1.83		

Index

Continued on next page

Index